Library of
Davidson College

Theories for Teaching

Theories for

Lindley J. Stiles, editor

*A Publication of the Center
for the Teaching Professions,
Northwestern University, in cooperation with the
W. K. Kellogg Foundation*

DODD, MEAD & COMPANY

Teaching

by

Joe Park, Sonja Stone, and William Barron
B. Claude Mathis and William McGaghie
Hugh G. Petrie
Paul Bohannan, William Powers,
 and Mark Schoepfle
David C. Epperson
Dolores E. Cross and Emilye Fields
Gustave J. Rath and Tom McAuliffe

New York   1974

371.1
S856t

COPYRIGHT © 1974 BY DODD, MEAD & COMPANY, INC.
ALL RIGHTS RESERVED

NO PART OF THIS BOOK MAY BE REPRODUCED IN ANY FORM
WITHOUT PERMISSION IN WRITING FROM THE PUBLISHER

ISBN: 0396-06905-3
LIBRARY OF CONGRESS CATALOG CARD NUMBER: 73-15030

PRINTED IN THE UNITED STATES OF AMERICA

DESIGNED BY JEFFREY M. BARRIE

Contents

PREFACE ix

Introduction
    LINDLEY J. STILES

1
Scientific Theory for Teaching: Its Nature and Role   9
    JOE PARK, SONJA STONE, AND WILLIAM BARRON

2
From Theories for Learning to Theories for Teaching   30
    B. CLAUDE MATHIS AND WILLIAM G. MC GAGHIE

3
The Believing in Seeing   51
    HUGH G. PETRIE

4
Systems Conflict in the Learning Alliance   76
    PAUL BOHANNAN, WILLIAM POWERS, AND MARK SCHOEPFLE

5
Assessing Alternative Teaching-Learning Alliances   97
    DAVID C. EPPERSON

6
Influence of Individual Differences on Instructional Theories   118
    DOLORES E. CROSS AND EMILYE FIELDS

7
A Systems Approach to the Theory for Teaching   139
    GUSTAVE J. RATH AND TOM MC AULIFFE

Index   171

Planning Committee

B. J. CHANDLER, Dean, School of Education, Northwestern University

B. CLAUDE MATHIS, Associate Dean, School of Education, and Director of the Center for the Teaching Professions, Northwestern University

LINDLEY J. STILES, Professor of Education for Interdisciplinary Studies, Sociology, and Political Science, Northwestern University

Authors

WILLIAM BARRON, Research Associate, Northwestern University

PAUL BOHANNAN, Professor of Anthropology and Education, Northwestern University

DOLORES E. CROSS, Assistant Professor of Education, Northwestern University

DAVID C. EPPERSON, Professor of Education and Urban Affairs, and Master of the College of Community Studies, Northwestern University

EMILYE FIELDS, Research Associate, Northwestern University

B. CLAUDE MATHIS, Associate Dean, School of Education, and Director of the Center for the Teaching Professions, Northwestern University

TOM MCAULIFFE, Research Associate, Northwestern University

WILLIAM C. MCGAGHIE, Research Associate, Northwestern University

JOE PARK, Professor of Education, Northwestern University

HUGH G. PETRIE, Associate Professor, Philosophy of Education, University of Illinois, Urbana-Champaign

WILLIAM POWERS, Research Associate, Northbrook, Illinois

GUSTAVE J. RATH, Professor, Industrial Engineering and Management Science, and Director of the Design and Development Center, Northwestern University

MARK SCHOEPFLE, Research Associate, Northwestern University

SONJA STONE, Research Associate, Northwestern University

Preface

The practice of teaching has long been limited by a lack of refined knowledge about the roles, goals, designs, and strategies of instruction. As a consequence, teachers still tend to teach as they themselves were taught, employing a minimum of critical analysis of the appropriateness of particular instructional procedures. Programs of preparation for teaching, likewise, in the absence of refined theoretical and research guidelines, typically aim to transmit to prospective teachers accumulated examples of the techniques that successful teachers have used. The apprenticeship, in which the neophyte learns to replicate the model of a master teacher, continues to be the primary means of developing new teaching personnel — for all ages and types of learners. Unfortunately, in all too many instances the models emulated are either ineffective or too individualistic to allow general adaptation by others. Thus, the process of learning to teach is largely one of trial-and-error in which new professionals may perpetuate the weaknesses as well as the strengths of their tutors without being aware of the differences.

Research on teaching is a relatively new area of human inquiry. Only in modern times have scholars begun to reject the folklore that teaching skill is inherited and, thus, incapable of being learned or objectively analyzed. Such research as has been undertaken, however, has been handicapped by a general failure to relate theory to formulated strategies. Without theoretical perspective, it is difficult to know which questions need answering or to know the meaning of the information accumulated about teaching. A few scholars, notably among them Jerome Bruner, have attempted to formulate a theory for teaching (or a theory for nonteaching, as Carl Rogers has done) . Others have argued that teaching and learning are so intertwined that they cannot be studied as separate processes. Such scholars generally subscribe to the superficial doctrine that "if learning does not occur, there has been no teaching." Thus, they claim, the focus should be on learning and not teaching. Others take the position that teaching is an art, rather than a systematically ordered process, and as such defies scientific investigation, discrete description, and general replication. Increasingly, however, scholars are coming to believe that teaching *can* be studied objectively as well as theoretically and that successful approaches and strategies can be identified and taught. As research on teaching is undertaken, the need is for refined theory to point the way.

This book, written by a team of scholars from various disciplines, aims to show how various kinds of theories can help to shape the nature and contributions of teaching. The authors write out of a common commitment that teaching is a process that is unique and discrete within itself, one that may function whether or not learning takes place and one, furthermore, that needs to be understood if it is to be improved. However, they approach their tasks from different perspectives and backgrounds of experience, with each author contributing unique insights into the ways that theories influence teaching. Together, they focus the reader's attention on the importance of theories for teaching and illustrate in a variety of ways the differences that given theories can make in the teaching approach and its effectiveness.

Dodd, Mead & Company is pleased to join with the Center for the Teaching Professions of Northwestern University and the W. K. Kellogg Foundation, which supports the Center's activities, in bringing this important publication to teachers and educators of teachers. The pioneering nature of the book, the practical impact of the ideas and insights presented in it, the enhancement of teaching as a professional process that it achieves — all make this book a signal venture.

LINDLEY J. STILES, Editor

Theories for Teaching

Introduction

LINDLEY J. STILES

How we teach is dependent, to some extent at least, on the theories we accept. Whatever the approach, the strategies employed, and the relationships generated, the choice is related to one or more theoretical constructs that may or may not be consciously identified. Nevertheless, many who teach are unaware of the roles that various theories play in their work. It is possible to teach by intuition and imitation—and to be reasonably successful—without having analyzed the beliefs and conceptions underlying the processes. In traditionally oriented educational institutions, teaching patterns tend to be passed from one generation to another without the benefits of reflective analysis or objective verification. Ironically, too, much of the research on teaching and the treatises on "how to teach" have given little attention to basic theories concerning the nature and effectiveness of teaching. As long as teaching is viewed as a monolithic process involving stereotyped goals, procedures, and relationships, it may appear to be removed from and impervious to theoretical influences. It is only when there is concern with the improvement of teaching, in substantial ways, that questions are confronted about the theories that undergird particular approaches and tactics in the teaching-learning processes.

That there is no single theory for teaching, one appropriate to all teachers and to every situation, the authors of this book unanimously agree. Some of us even doubt that it will ever be possible to construct a common theory that will serve all teachers equally well. Our study of this problem has convinced us that what is involved is an interplay of multiple theories that relate to such matters as goals of education; how learning takes place; the traits and motivations of individual students; teacher-student relationships; why and how results are assessed; and, of course, the nature of teaching itself. Also to be considered are theories about how to organize instruction in an institutional setting to make maximum use of both human talents and technological resources. The professional life style of the individual teacher, as well as the point of view he holds about goals and commitments, represents another category of theories that may influence teaching. The authors concur that what is needed and appropriate, in this stage of the development of the art and science of teaching, is for all those who are interested in improving their pedagogical effectiveness to focus on theories *for* teaching rather than on a theory or theories *of* teaching. The challenge for all, regardless of age level of students or skills or subjects taught, is to analyze the contributions that different theories can make to teaching. The goal is to develop a professional foundation for selecting alternative strategies for promoting learning in particular situations with specific learners. To help with this task is one of the key purposes of this book. A secondary aim is to stimulate scholars and researchers to give more attention to the plurality of influences that various theories may exert on teaching.

Sponsored by the Center for the Teaching Professions

The development and publication of this book was sponsored by the Center for the Teaching Professions at Northwestern University. The Center itself was established in the fall of 1969 with support from the W. K. Kellogg Foundation of Battle Creek, Michigan. Its function is to stimulate the improvement of teaching—particularly within the various professions and in colleges and universities—by its own activities and by serving as a model for other institutions. The Center was conceived out of an awareness that of the three key ways that professions maintain and advance themselves—namely, *teaching, practice,* and *research*—teaching has been the most neglected function. When a profession does a poor job of teaching its future members or practitioners in service, it nurtures a weakness that, in terms of its overall impact, no amount of inspired and dedicated individual performance or creative research can counteract. Thus, to improve

Introduction 3

a profession, the first priority must be to improve the effectiveness of its teaching. And because professional training is built upon the learning that has taken place at pre-professional levels, members of a profession must be concerned, also, with the effectiveness of teaching in elementary and secondary schools, as well as in undergraduate colleges.

This book is one of a number of projects sponsored by the Center for the Teaching Professions that aim to focus attention and effort on the improvement of teaching. An earlier publication was *Profiles in College Teaching* (1972), edited by B. Claude Mathis and William C. McGaghie, and written by outstanding teachers of different subjects at Northwestern University. A symposium on the "Teaching of English" was sponsored by the Center in October, 1972. In November of that year, an invitational conference on the theme, "The Improvement of Teaching in Higher Education," brought representatives of the various professions from across the nation to study this problem. A conference on "Course and Teacher Evaluation" that drew national and multiprofessional participation was held in the spring of 1973.

On the campus of Northwestern University, the Center has stimulated widespread interest in the improvement of teaching in colleges and professional schools. The Graduate School of Management and Dental School faculties have become totally involved in efforts to evaluate and improve pre-service and in-service teaching programs for professionals in their respective fields. Other departments and schools are engaged in special thrusts toward this objective. Another type of project sponsored by the Center has been the recruitment of faculty fellows from different professional specializations for a year's training in teaching. The strategy to which the Center is committed is, first, to involve Northwestern University departments and schools in the improvement of teaching and, then, to spread interest engendered to other institutions and professional groups.

Interdisciplinary Authorship

The authors of this book represent various academic disciplines and professional fields. Each has unique interests and has had extensive experience related to theoretical constructs for teaching. The academic and professional fields represented include anthropology, education, engineering, higher education, philosophy, political science, psychology, and sociology. Included among the authors are scholars of international renown in their fields of specialization who have taken time to investigate teaching as well. Included also are a number of younger scholars studying at Northwestern University, each of whom has brought to the work a dedication to improving teaching. Younger authors, particularly, exerted a strong influence on the development of this volume through their discontent with the status quo of teaching and through the probing questions they asked about how various theories might influence its improvement. That the mix of disciplines and scholars—as well as of ages, sex, racial and ethnic background—proved to be a most healthy one, is reflected in the results.

A Team Process

As unique as the mix of authorship was the process by which this book was written. Team and cooperative procedures were utilized throughout, with each participant having a chance to help conceive the format for the book and to influence the development and evaluation of the various chapters.

Work on the book began with the Planning Committee's selection of the professors who were to be invited to participate in the project. Each professor was urged to invite one or more younger scholars to join in the work. The conceptual phase of the book was carried on during a series of weekly meetings at which different dimensions of theories for teaching were considered. Chapters proposed by the various writing teams, each of which represented an expression of the interests and scholarship of those involved, were considered and evaluated by the entire group. Discussions were recorded and transcribed as aids to authors. A highlight of this phase of the effort was the mind rubbing that went on as scholars from different disciplines developed understandings and appreciations of each other's ideas. At first, it must be admitted, the differences among members of the group seemed so great that we wondered if we could ever put our ideas together in a cohesive volume. However, our difficulties in understanding each other became minimized when we realized that, although we were using different terminology to express our ideas, we were talking about many of the same ideas. After we learned how to translate each other's professional jargon into a common language, we were able to think together productively about how various theories can influence teaching.

Subsequent to the conceptualization of the book and its different chapters by the group as a whole, author teams undertook the writing of the chapters. As each chapter was completed in preliminary draft, it was duplicated and distributed to all involved in the project. Each writing team met with the entire group to discuss its efforts and to receive criticisms and suggestions. Following the group assessments, writing teams rewrote their chapters—each being free to incorporate or reject, as their scholarship dictated, the suggestions of their fellow authors.

A final stage of the process was the editing of the manuscript into a unified whole. The edited version was then duplicated and distributed again to all involved in the project and a final evaluation and "group editing" session held. Changes suggested were incorporated by the editor in the final draft. Additional editorial treatment came from Dodd, Mead & Company, Inc., publishers and distributors of the book.

Thus, this book has had the benefit of the thinking and scholarship of many different authors, each being a part of the whole but responsible for a specific chapter. Yet authors were not limited by the opinions of others in the group, nor was an attempt made to achieve consensus. The aim of the group process, rather, was to generate a healthy intermeshing of interdisciplinary scholarship without restricting the creativity and commitments of the various specialists involved.

Significantly, our ideas about the role of theory in teaching changed as we learned together. We started out, for example, with the idea that we could possibly formulate a theory for teaching that would postulate how all teaching might be carried out. Early deliberations convinced us that we had to think of multiple theories that would prescribe differing approaches. Ultimately, we came to agree that we had to write about theories *for* teaching since, in reality, the theories that influence pedagogical practice are drawn from a variety of sources. The teaching that results from their use is dependent upon the alternatives selected.

Overview of Content

Briefly, Chapters 1 and 2 present an analysis of the relevance of the scientific method, and of the contributions of different theories of learning to the study and improvement of teaching. Chapters 3 and 4 show how theories from other disciplines—such as anthropology, philosophy, and psychotherapy—can be utilized to increase our understanding of the teaching processes. Chapters 5, 6, and 7 make applications of particular theories to illustrate how they influence teaching performance.

As a foundation for our thinking about how different theories may influence teaching, Dr. Joe Park, Sonja Stone, and William Barron present in Chapter 1 an analysis of the nature and role of theory itself, with particular reference to the interactions that develop between natural and human phenomena. A key question confronted in this chapter is whether theories for teaching must be wholly objective, in a scientific sense, or will of necessity be partially subjective. The focus throughout the chapter is on the larger question: "Can theory guide practice?" To the extent that it can, the authors conclude, it is possible to predict the consequence of selected alternatives to teaching.

Dr. B. Claude Mathis and William C. McGaghie report, in Chapter 2, on how theories of learning can influence teaching performance. In particular, they review efforts of scholars to build theories about teaching and review the key conceptions of human learning that undergird different teaching tactics. In their interpretations of the implications of psychological theories for teaching, they raise important questions about whether any system of behavioral analysis can provide all the answers for an approach to the teaching-learning process.

The interactions between perception and teaching are analyzed by Dr. Hugh G. Petrie in Chapter 3. He shows how both teachers and students need to be trained in perception and illustrates how the learning alliance fails when the perceptual hierarchies of teacher and taught do not mesh. The currently popular belief that behavioral objectives and teaching strategies can be precisely determined in advance to assure predicted results is questioned by the author, yet

Introduction

the importance of goals for teaching receives his support. Throughout the chapter, experience and the affective reactions of students are seen as intertwined with the cognitive development that a teacher may aim to promote.

The "learning alliance" is a new term conceived by Dr. Paul Bohannan, William Powers, and Mark Schoepfle to describe the teaching-learning relationship. In Chapter 4 they analyze the similarities and differences in three types of alliance: the therapeutic, as practiced by psychoanalysts; the ethnographic, employed by anthropologists in dealing with informants; and the learning alliance, employed by teachers. The authors show how the learning alliance can function only if the teacher is sensitive to conflicts that may prevail between social, institutional, and professional goals and those pursued by students. Suggested bargain-making techniques for maintaining consonance, and thus the learning alliance itself, are discussed.

In Chapter 5, Dr. David C. Epperson develops a unique format for analyzing the impact of various alternative teaching-learning alliances on human behavior. The idea that each teacher must deal with learner discontent and does so in terms of particular perspectives of human behavior and individual resourcefulness opens new vistas of teaching choices for exploration. Particularly useful to researchers as well as teachers will be the criteria the author formulates for evaluating alternative perspectives of the learning alliance.

How individual differences—in both students and teachers—influence approaches and strategies of teaching is the focus of Chapter 6, by Dr. Dolores E. Cross and Emilye Fields. The values placed on differences, and the social pressures to maintain or obliterate them, are seen as factors in the divergent responses made by teachers as well as others. Analyses are presented of the classroom structures that take into account the differences that typically prevail in a group of students. Interpersonal techniques that teachers may employ to respond to individual differences are identified.

A final chapter, prepared by Dr. Gustave J. Rath and Tom McAuliffe applies systems analysis theory and techniques to the kind of decision making that constantly confronts all who teach. Illustrations are presented to show how a teacher and students determine goals, select resources, develop alternative learning activities, and evaluate outcomes. This type of model building for teaching is shown to be the link between theory and scientific method : theory provides direction, while scientific procedures sharpen perceptions. An assumption is made in Chapter 7 that, in teaching, reliance is placed on scientific processes to generate valid information about the classroom and the students in it. Added reality is given to the systems strategy, a process of problem solving, by using it to analyze the preceding chapters of this book. How theory is used in systems analysis is shown and, conversely, how systems analysis can be employed to test the validity of theories for teaching. A final section discusses the requirements and specifications of the theory for teaching. The chapter and the book conclude with a quotation from Kurt Lewin which—as far as the improvement of teaching is concerned and despite our inability to formulate a definitive theory for teaching—all involved in this project can readily endorse : "there is nothing as practical as a good theory."

1 Scientific Theory for Teaching: Its Nature and Role

JOE PARK, SONJA STONE, and WILLIAM BARRON

> Theory of what is and theory of what ought to be are perpetually confused. THE OXFORD ENGLISH DICTIONARY

Some animals, such as the wolf and chimpanzee, teach their young, as Farley Mowat [1] and Jane Van Lawick-Goodall [2] have so carefully observed—but only man theorizes. Certainly he is the only animal who verbalizes his theories, writes them down, and deliberately and systematically reformulates them as his experience warrants. In addition, as has been noted by such authors as Thomas Kuhn [3] and Michael Polanyi,[4] all of man's knowledge is theory-laden. Whether it is implicit or explicit, theory is a necessary component of all knowledge. Implicit in our approach to this chapter is a certain predisposition which we attribute to our training in philosophy. Accordingly, we neither endorse nor reject specific theories for teaching. Instead, we raise certain questions about the very enterprise of theory building, particularly as it relates to teaching. Thus, in a sense, this is an exercise in meta-theory.

---

[1] Farley Mowat, *Never Cry Wolf* (Boston: Little, Brown and Company, 1963), pp. 209–218.
[2] Jane Van Lawick-Goodall, *In the Shadow of Man* (Boston: Houghton Mifflin Company, 1971), p. 168.
[3] Thomas S. Kuhn, *The Structure of Scientific Revolutions* (Chicago: University of Chicago Press, 1962).
[4] Michael Polanyi, *Personal Knowledge* (New York: Harper and Row, Publishers, Torchbook, 1964).

Initially, many of us may feel more comfortable in the context of implicit than explicit theory. To the extent that our choices, actions, and decisions are guided by some frame of reference, we all operate on a theoretical level. Regardless of our level of sophistication or expertise in auto mechanics, electronics, or economics, we manipulate cars, television sets, and budgets according to sound theoretical principles. On the other hand, these principles (however vague to us as laymen) are, for the physicist or economist, explicit. Similarly, as educators, we frequently impart facts, values, and skills without fully understanding their theoretical foundations. Presumably, then, one of the functions of educational theorists is to clarify existing theories for teaching—often implicit in their various guises and dimensions. But another, perhaps more important, function is to develop new and explicit theories for teaching.

In the process of theorizing, hunches and beliefs are converted into hypotheses and propositions to be tested and validated. Sometimes this is achieved through empirical research, but logic is also employed to expose and evaluate assumptions and inferences as well as to dispose of fallacies and trivia. Facts are assessed in terms of relevance and classified accordingly. Now, hunches, beliefs, assumptions, inferences, and even facts are but the raw material of theory, while logic and empirical research are its tools. Ultimately, according to Abraham Kaplan: "A theory is a symbolic construction . . . thus contrasted both with practice and with fact . . . the device for interpreting, criticizing, and unifying established laws, modifying them to fit data unanticipated in their formulation, and guiding the enterprise of discovering new and more powerful generalizations."[5] Although Kaplan's definition of theory is carefully constructed and easily comprehended, it is by no means universally accepted. The eternal problem of defining theory is, therefore, one of the recurring concerns of this chapter.

Inasmuch as education is classified as one of the disciplines within the social sciences, it falls heir to some of the difficulties in social science theory. Nonetheless, it is somewhat paradoxical that education is not only a discipline unto itself but it is also the vehicle through

---

[5] Abraham Kaplan, *The Conduct of Inquiry* (San Francisco: Chandler Publishing Company, 1964), pp. 295–297.

which all disciplines are transmitted. Thus, while education may share some of the liabilities of the social sciences, it must also claim some of the laurels of the physical sciences.

During the last decade certain philosophers have expended considerable effort in analyzing the teaching concept.[6] While their efforts have been praiseworthy and productive of a certain degree of clarity, it is still the case that the concept remains vague. That is to say, there are no sharp boundary lines that can be drawn to mark off teaching from things we would not want to call teaching. In other words, there remains a penumbra in which it is not at all clear whether the word "teaching" applies. Possibly, most would agree that teaching includes helping children learn what is thought important. But suppose a person called a teacher grasps a child, shakes him, and shouts at him in an effort to get him to remember that 7 x 8 = 56. Is that teaching? Apparently, some would say that it was. Others would not. If a history teacher lies to his students in order to promote the belief that our forefathers were paragons of virtue and wisdom, is that teaching? Some would argue that this was propagandizing and falls outside the realm of teaching. Others proud to call themselves teachers have lied to their students and have called it teaching. Suppose a biology teacher interrupts a child who is carefully examining the anatomy of a fly captured in the classroom, in order to focus the child's attention on the textbook assignment on the nemertean, is that teaching? A Charles Silberman might not wish to consider it so, but apparently some teachers consider their chief functions to be the giving of assignments, the hearing of recitations, and testing for facts retained from the study of a textbook.

If the illustrations have made the point intended, we shall have to live with the vagueness of the concept. About all we can say is that teaching is an activity [7] carried on by a person we call a teacher, which is intended to get another person (or help another person) called a student or pupil, to learn something. One or both parties may think

---

[6] Thomas F. Green, *The Activities of Teaching* (New York: McGraw-Hill Book Company, 1971).

[7] It must be remembered that teaching does not always refer to an activity. Sometimes we speak of teaching and refer to a body of knowledge. On other occasions we speak of teaching and mean a profession or occupation.

the material to be learned important for reasons that may or may not be intrinsic to the material. It is generally agreed, however, that learning is most likely to occur when both parties accept the significance of that which is being taught.

Theory (from the Greek word *Theoria*) is defined as an act of viewing, contemplating, considering, and arranging what we know in some way that makes possible description, prescription, prediction, explanation, and the systematic testing of ideas. While this may do as a general definition, it is, like any other definition of theory, vague. Again we do not know exactly where to draw the line between what is theory and what is not theory. Most certainly this is the case with respect to what persons would call a theory for teaching. To minimize the vagueness and confusion which surround the concepts of theory and teaching, then, it may be expedient to confine our discussion to scientific theories for teaching. On the other hand, we cannot ignore the fact that, historically, some of the most influential educational theorists were not scientists in the "hard" contemporary sense of the word. Briefly, then, we must acknowledge the nature and significance of "non scientific" theories for teaching. Heading this list is Plato's *Republic,* which is the classic statement of Western pedagogy as well as of speculative societies.

In the physical sciences, theory is generally understood as systematic formulation of laws or law-like statements which purport to explain natural phenomena. While philosophers of science and mathematics tend to subscribe to this definition, their colleagues in ethics, metaphysics, and epistemology work with a different genre of theory. For example, epistemology, or theory of knowledge, is basically an inquiry into such questions as "What is knowledge?" "What does it mean to have knowledge?" and "What constitutes proof of knowledge?" Hence, one kind of "nonscientific" theory is philosophical theory, which, in good Socratic fashion, generates more questions than laws.

After countless mutations, the Socratic tradition has produced numerous movements, including one which is now known as analytic philosophy and which has deliberately and self-consciously emulated contemporary scientific methods of inquiry. C. D. Broad described this school of analytic or critical philosophy as ". . . a science which shall try to analyze and define the concepts which are used in daily life and in the special sciences. Whilst all the special sciences *use* these concepts, none of them is *about* these concepts as such. I regard Critical Philosophy as the science which has this for its most fundamental task."[8] One of the foremost analytic philosophers was Bertrand Russell, who also wrote extensively in the area of educational theory.

Within the evolving Western philosophic tradition, there is also a group known as speculative philosophers, whose ranks include such pedagogical giants as Rousseau and Dewey. Thus, another kind of "nonscientific" theory is speculative philosophy, which, according to Broad, is concerned with "the nature of Reality as a whole, and . . . the position and prospects of men in it."[9] As a classic work in speculative philosophy, Plato's *Republic* can be nicely contrasted with Gilbert Ryle's *Concept of Mind,* a popular example of analytic philosophy. The *Republic* is, of course, a monumental effort to synthesize Plato's theory of "what is" with "what ought to be." Ryle, simulating the technique of reduction, effectively "decomposes" the Cartesian concept of mind. Needless to say, the philosophical analysis of the mind has far-reaching implications for teaching theory. While Plato's vision was macroscopic, Ryle's was microscopic. But before carrying these distinctions too far, we should stress the fact that most philosophers are both speculative and critical. Plato was both, as were Russell and Dewey; so is Ryle. The excesses of unbridled imagination are no less dangerous than what Martin Luther King called the "paralysis of analysis."

Having paid our respects to the vast body of "non scientific" theory, we now turn to scientific theory.

Scientific Theories for Teaching

It is probably not an exaggeration to say that no one doubts the success of chemists and physicists in acquiring more and more know-

---

[8] C. D. Broad, "Critical and Speculative Philosophy," in *Contemporary British Philosophy,* ed. J. H. Muirhead, 1st Series (New York: The Macmillan Company, 1924), p. 83.
[9] *Ibid.,* p. 96.

ledge of the natural world. The perfection of the methods and principles of the natural sciences has definitely enabled mankind to discard many of the myths of earlier times, thereby enabling people to control much of the physical environment for the first time. In fact, our modern age has often justifiably been called the age of science. Indeed the successes of natural scientists have established a standard for all knowledge; few people today will accept anything as true which does not have the certitude of scientific research.

In accounting for the accomplishments of the physical sciences, many individuals have given the credit to the method and principles of these sciences. It is, therefore, no wonder that many attempts on the part of educators to gain the same depth and breadth of knowledge as the natural sciences possess have been based largely upon the application of scientific methods and principles to their own field. Of course the emphasis upon the application of scientific techniques to other areas did not originate with education. Beginning from the seventeenth and eighteenth centuries, thinkers of all disciplines have heralded the use of scientific principles in their respective areas. This notable group stems from the seventeenth-century philosopher John Locke and extends to the modern-day psychologist B. F. Skinner. Yet it is not at all clear that all these innovators would have shared the same concept of the basic underlying principles of science. It would be advantageous, therefore, to outline briefly the most commonly accepted view of scientific theory.[10]

Many philosophers of science are advocates of the hypothetico-deductive model of scientific theory, of which the important elements are deductive form, falsifiability, and predictive capacity.[11] The hypothetico-deductive model of explanation purports to be a model

---

[10] Perhaps it should be mentioned before discussing the hypothetico-deductive model of scientific theory that it is not without rivals. For one example, see Norwood Hanson, *The Pattern of Discovery: An Inquiring into the Conceptual Foundations of Science* (Cambridge, Mass.; University Press, 1958).

[11] This model cannot be fully explained in this brief chapter. See, for example, K. R. Popper, *The Logic of Scientific Discovery* (London: Hutchinson and Co., 1959) or C. G. Hempel, *Aspects of Scientific Explanation* (New York and Glencoe, Ill.: The Free Press, 1965).

of all causal explanation.[12] To cite a case as an explanation of an event is to cite, at least implicitly, an instance of a general law. The hypothetico-deductive model is based upon the use of this general law and the initial conditions (the particular circumstances which precede the event to be explained) as the premises of a deductive argument from which the event to be causally explained is logically deduced in accordance with the laws of deductive logic. The form of the hypothetico-deductive model is given by this schema:

$$\frac{L_1, L_2, \ldots L_n}{C_1, C_2, \ldots C_n}$$
$$E$$

where $L_1, L_2, \ldots L_n$ are general laws; $C_1, C_2, \ldots C_n$ are the initial conditions of particular fact; and the horizontal line depicts that E, the event to be explained, follows as a logical conclusion.

As based upon the hypothetico-deductive model of explanation, a scientific theory is similarly a set of deductively connected laws. The laws that explain individual events are axioms of the theory. The laws that are explained by other laws are the theorems of the theory. Scientific theory thus has the same deductive form as the explanation of events. Axioms are designated by their place in the theory, so that while laws may be axioms in one theory, they are theorems in another theory. For example, the axioms in Galileo's theory of freely falling bodies on earth become theorems of Newton's theory of universal gravitation.

Before bringing this brief discussion of the hypothetico-deductive model of scientific theory to a close, two final points need to be mentioned. First, although the deductive aspect of this model has been dealt with, the hypothetico aspect has yet to be covered. As clearly seen by Popper,[13] the status of the general laws of scientific theory is that of falsifiable hypotheses. The concept of falsifiability denotes the fact that from any general law in a scientific theory, *empirical* (observable) consequences can be drawn. These empirical consequences

---

[12] C. G. Hempel and Paul Oppenheim, "The Logic of Explanation," *Philosophy of Science,* Vol. 15 (April, 1948), pp. 135–175.
[13] Popper, *op. cit.*

serve as a means of testing the general laws since the anticipated consequences can be compared with the facts produced by experimentation. In other words, to do science in this manner is to have hypotheses that are refutable. Secondly, as suggested by the idea of drawing consequences from general laws, scientific theory enables prediction of events. In fact, prediction, just like explanation, is merely the deductive inference of a particular event from the initial conditions and general laws of a scientific theory. Prediction and explanation are therefore symmetrical, the only difference being in the previously unknown status of predicted events as opposed to the previously known status of explained events. In summary then, the three important elements of the hypothetico-deductive model of scientific theory are (1) deductive form, (2) falsifiability, and (3) predictive capacity.

The Objective Viewpoint of a Scientific Theory for Teaching

While many social scientists have openly advocated the adoption of scientific theory within their respective disciplines, some of these individuals have gone one step further in the parallels they have drawn between the natural and social sciences. This additional parallel concerns the nature of the phenomena to be studied: for at least methodological purposes the claim is made that there is no difference in kind between natural phenomena and human phenomena. The basic tenets of this position were formulated by J. S. Mill as long ago as his writing of the *System of Logic* [14] in 1843. Since for Mill the only phenomena which can be studied adequately are those that exhibit regular patterns of behavior, the study of human phenomena must limit itself to consideration of the observable patterns on human behavior. No consideration of unobservable, irregular aspects of human phenomena is thought to be possible; hence, questions of human intention, purpose, and meaning are left to others or in some cases (e.g., as occasionally suggested by the radical behaviorist John B. Watson) [15] denied as legitimate questions. Thus, for a number of social scientists there is no essential difference between the social sciences and the natural sciences.

---

[14] J. S. Mill, *System of Logic* (New York: Longmans, Green and Co., 1947).
[15] J. B. Watson, "Psychology as the Behaviorist Views It," *Psychological Review*, Vol. 20 (1913), pp. 158–177.

For those social scientists who adopt the belief in the fundamental similarity between the natural and human phenomena which can be studied, there immediately follows a vitally important narrowing of viewpoint. The limitation of human phenomena to observable patterns of regular behavior eliminates any description of the human subject's own experience, thereby limiting the scientist's viewpoint to the description of his and his co-observers' experiences of their common object of experience, human behavior. This methodological viewpoint can be appropriately termed the objective viewpoint,[16] since its sole concern is with a scientist's observation of an object. Objective, in the sense of objective viewpoint, is based on the distinction between public and private events and the fact that public events can only be experienced by observers of such events, while private events can only be directly experienced by individual human beings.[17] Description in the objective viewpoint can only be defined in terms of the observer's frame of reference. The use of empathy or other similar techniques as a basis for describing the experience of the observed subject within his own viewpoint is not utilized; instead, the scientist describes his observations in terms of his own scientific viewpoint.

In an essay on the theoretical foundation of his concept of behaviorism, Skinner states his conceptualization of the objective viewpoint:

> An adequate science of behavior must consider events taking place within the skin of the organism, not as physiological mediators of behavior (or it might be added as intentional acts), but as part of behavior itself. It can deal with these events without assuming that they have any special nature or must be known in any special way. The skin is not that important as a boundary. Private and public events have the same kinds of physical dimensions.[18]

---

[16] A "viewpoint as used here can be either objective or subjective and still be compatible with the above-mentioned hypothetico-deductive model of scientific theory.

[17] This use of the term "objective viewpoint" is intended to make no reference whatsoever to the common use of the term "objective" to mean bias-free, as contrasted with "subjective" used to mean biased.

[18] B. F. Skinner, "Behaviorism at Fifty," in *Behaviorism and Phenomenology,* ed. T. W. Wann (Chicago: University of Chicago Press, 1964), p. 84.

Skinner likewise says that he is a radical behaviorist in the sense that he finds no place in his theories for anything which is mental.[19] Skinner is therefore committed to a description of teaching in terms of the objective standpoint: examination of teaching behavior as it can be categorized in terms of his own conceptual schema without any consideration of the teacher's viewpoint (i.e., his own meanings, purposes, and intentions).

Skinner's theory for teaching is a scientific theory of the objective viewpoint built upon the psychological law of reinforcement.[20] "We have made sure that the effects do occur," he tells us, "and that they occur under conditions which are optimal for producing the changes called learning." As a result of these behaviorist studies, we are now able to maintain behavior in given states of strength for long periods of time in pigeons, rats monkeys, dogs, and children. Skinner further maintains that results of laboratory experimentation make possible the extrapolation of results to daily life.

In other words, we have arrived, in the opinion of Skinner, at the "exciting prospect" of advancing human learning—if only we could improve the technology of teaching. Skinner believes this can be accomplished if we turn from the aversive controls that have marked the course of education, to positive reinforcement. This would entail a thorough revision of classroom practices and the utilization of behavioral modification techniques. The whole process should be able to be directed at competence in any field. For this to be accomplished, the subject matter important enough to be mastered must be divided into a very large number of small steps. The learner must then be positively reinforced along each step of his learning experience and, of course, this can best be done on most occasions by a teaching machine, which would leave the teacher free to give personal attention to the learner.

Skinner recognizes that if his techniques are adopted, the cry will be heard across the land that the child is being conditioned rather than educated. It is true, he points out, that the materials and techniques developed are not designed to "train the mind" nor further some

---

[19] *Ibid.*, p. 106.
[20] *The Technology of Teaching* (New York: Appleton-Century-Crofts, 1968).

vague "understanding of mathematics." Instead, they are to be used to give the child a genuine competence in reading, writing, spelling, and arithmetic. Once these skills are acquired by the use of machines, then the teacher may begin to function as an "intellectual, cultural, and emotional contact of that distinct sort which testify to her status as a human being." Yet, ironically, Skinner's theory of teaching is unable to discuss more fully these types of teaching contact with students because of his adoption of a purely objective viewpoint. Skinner does, nonetheless, provide a scientific theory for teaching which rests upon the psychological law of reinforcement and the invention of the teaching machine.

The Subjective Viewpoint of a Scientific Theory for Teaching

Many social scientists have adopted an approach to their studies substantially different from that of the objectivists. This different viewpoint stems from the refusal to consider natural phenomena and human phenomena as essentially of the same kind. The objectivists' belief in a parallel between natural and human phenomena is considered as ignoring a vital aspect of human phenomena. Those scientists adopting the subjective viewpoint believe human phenomena to have a metaphorical "inside" which can be scientifically studied, in addition to an "outside," regular pattern of observable behavior. Human beings endow their actions with meaning (i.e., they have emotions, attitudes, purposes, ends, and intentions), whereas the phenomena into which the natural scientists inquire may be said to be essentially meaningless. The social sciences including education thus require the study of an additional dimension, human meaning, which is not required in the study of the natural sciences.

The clearest expression of this viewpoint is made by Max Weber in his description of his study of sociological phenomena:

> Sociology . . . is a science which attempts the interpretive understanding of social action in order thereby to arrive at a causal explanation of its cause and effects. In "action" is included all human behavior when and in so far as the acting individual attaches a subjective meaning to it. Action in this sense may be either overt or purely inward or subjective; it may consist of positive intervention in a situation, or of deliberately

refraining from such intervention or passively acquiescing in the situation.²¹

It follows from the imputation of meaning to human phenomena that the objective viewpoint must be augmented by a subjective viewpoint. The observed subject's frame of reference becomes vitally important and his action must now be described in terms of the meanings with which he understands his own actions. In other words, in contrast to description from the objective viewpoint, description from the subjective viewpoint is defined in terms of the observed subject's own meaningful experience. The action of the observed subject becomes intelligible when the scientific observer has come to understand the meanings with which the observed subject endows his action. The means of achieving this scientific task is empathy, or to adopt Carl Rogers' term, "interpersonal knowing." ²² This technique enables the scientist to describe the actions of the observed subject within the framework of the subject's own viewpoint.

Carl Rogers' scientific theory for teaching as expressed in *Freedom to Learn* utilizes the subjective viewpoint to capture the meaning of the teaching experience. But before discussing this theory of teaching, the possible criticism that Rogers' subjective viewpoint precludes his theory from being considered scientific, must be answered. Throughout his various works Rogers states that he is proposing scientific hypotheses which presumably are falsifiable and allow for predictions.²³ While his theories do not have an explicitly deductive form, they could no doubt be transformed into deductive form without any loss of content. Furthermore, Rogers mentions at least two empirical criteria for his technique of interpersonal knowing—confirmation by the individual and consensual validation—which eliminate any notion that interpersonal knowing is a type of mystical process.²⁴

---

[21] Max Weber, *The Theory of Social and Economic Organization* (New York: Oxford University Press, 1947), p. 88.
[22] C. R. Rogers, "Toward a Science of the Person," in *Behaviorism and Phenomenology*, ed. T. W. Wann (Chicago: University of Chicago Press, 1964), p. 115.
[23] *Ibid.*, p. 116.
[24] *Ibid.*, p. 116.

Rogers' theory for teaching begins with the belief that within each infant occurs an organismic valuing process, in which each element and moment of what he is experiencing is weighed, selected, or rejected—depending upon whether it tends to actualize the organism or not. But what happens is that adults interfere and the child introjects the values of others. These introjected values lead to all sorts of disastrous consequences—not the least of which is the divorcing of ourselves from ourselves—that is, the individual begins to see a discrepancy between his organismically derived concepts and that which he is experiencing about him. If we would allow the child's organismic valuing mechanism to continue to function uninhibited, then, Rogers believes, a human being would evolve that would "tend to value those objects, experiences, and goals which contribute to his own survival, growth, and development, and to the survival and development of others." Thus, it is supposed, saving the human race from many of its present miseries.

Since the individual has this organismic valuing mechanism, the function of a teacher is not to tell the student what he should learn, but to help the student to select what he wants to learn. Instead of instructing another in what he must know, the teacher becomes a facilitator of learning and personal and social change by assisting the developing person at those points where help is requested. Since Rogers is offering hypotheses, they are meant to be dealt with empirically and not simply as prescription. And to the extent that his hypotheses are refutable, Rogers has established an avenue by which we can advance our scientific knowledge about facilitating learning.[25]

The contrast between the objective and subjective viewpoints of a scientific theory for teaching raises a significant question: "Are these two viewpoints and their correlative theories for teaching compatible?" While some extremists of both viewpoints sometimes deny the efficacy of the other's approach, we would maintain that, far from contradicting one another, these two viewpoints are complementary and both are necessary if there is to be a full account of teaching. Not all inquiry

---

[25] Carl Rogers, *Freedom to Learn: A View of What Education Might Become* (Columbus, Ohio: C. E. Merrill Publishing Co., 1969).

into teaching need be or should be completely objective or subjective.

B. F. Skinner's objective theory for teaching demonstrates the potential significance that the psychological theory of reinforcement has for the teaching of skills. His theory for teaching can allow for more effective use of the teacher's individual talents by freeing him from the tedious task of instilling basic skills. Also, the student is able to learn the basic skills faster and easier as a result of Skinner's proposed division of labor. Skinner's theory for teaching of the basic skills can easily be empirically tested and either confirmed or disconfirmed by simply employing his suggestion in the classroom.

On the other hand, Rogers' theory for teaching does not have equal adaptability to scientific verification. The development of science has not resulted in the same standards for easy testing of the meanings of human experience. In particular, Rogers' theory of facilitation, as it is based upon an underlying scientific theory of value, would be very difficult to test empirically. Nevertheless, Rogers' theory for teaching is valuable despite the lack of simple verificational procedures, if for no other reason than its attempt to capture the teaching experience in terms of the teacher's own framework of meaning. Rogers' adoption of the subjective viewpoint is no doubt one reason for the popularity of his ideas. Very few, if any, teachers are ready or willing to ignore the values, purposes, and intentions of their own experience.

Perhaps this comparison of the objective and subjective viewpoints of scientific theories of learning can best be seen as a call for more theories of both viewpoints and an improvement of the techniques for testing the theories of the subjective viewpoint, as well as expressing the need for educators who are willing to test the theories. But not even with more theories of both viewpoints and their empirical testing can one expect a final answer to the problem of teaching. As the needs of society and individuals change through time and as significant individual differences are considered, it becomes apparent that scientific theories for teaching can at best serve as a guide to teaching and not as an ultimate solution to the many problems facing a teacher. But it is precisely at the point of expecting theory to guide practice that an important problem arises: "Can theory guide practice?"

The Role of Theory in Practice

In order to consider the question raised above, we first need to observe that the physical scientist conceives of his role as that of advancing knowledge. That is, he seeks to develop testable theories with explanatory and predictive powers. Others, in turn, may use his theories for more practical purposes such as the exploration of outer space, the development of mighty machines of destruction, or the construction of gadgets for the entertainment of the masses.

But a successful and self-respecting physical scientist, *qua* pure theoretical scientist, would neither conceive of his role as that of studying values nor as that of prescribing what ought to be done with his theories. After all, his sole job as a scientist is to advance knowledge. Nevertheless, he will operate from certain value premises, just as any other human being does. Because of the values he holds about human life, for example, he may become alarmed at the ends to which his theories are put. Some nuclear physicists have undertaken to stop the construction and stockpiling of death-dealing implements of war, and some biochemists have voiced fears lest their findings regarding cloning be used for evil purposes by ambitious politicians. The scientists would, however, undoubtedly consider this kind of activity as outside the realm of theoretical physical science. He would probably think of himself as having been transported into another realm of activity and thought, namely that of normative judgments.

The social scientist, like his counterpart in the physical sciences, attempts to keep the wall of separation between "what is" and "what ought to be" high and unbreached. Nevertheless, some social scientists, *qua* social scientists, feel themselves rightfully and naturally conveyed into the realm of "what ought to be." For example, the late Robert Redfield, a noted anthropologist at the University of Chicago, defined the social sciences as "a group of disciplines that provide descriptions of human nature, human activity, and human institutions. . . . They strive for descriptions that are more illuminating, valid and comprehensive than are the corresponding descriptions of common sense." [26]

[26] Robert Redfield, "The Social Uses of Social Science," in *Teaching the Social Studies: What, Why, and How,* ed. Richard F. Gross, Walter E. McPhie

According to Redfield, the social sciences are analytical rather than historical and are used to understand a social problem or describe the "general characteristics of some class of social phenomena." [27]

So far Redfield's position does not appear to differ from that of the physical scientist. According to his view, both the physical scientist and the social scientist seek to discover, explain, describe, and test. Neither conceives of science as a search for *oughts*. But Redfield noticed a difference between the social and physical sciences at the point of practical application which, if correct, is of tremendous importance. He maintained that the findings of social science have to do with the "proving and the making of social values," even "the most ultimate values of society." [28]

It is true that every scientist influences the values of his society and vice versa. The scientist's dedication to the advancement of knowledge itself reflects an underlying value system—that is, that knowledge is valuable or that we "ought to" have knowledge. There are cultures in which the advancement of knowledge is not valued. All science is value-laden inasmuch as the basic values of the scientific endeavor are honesty, objectivity, accuracy, and humility before the facts. These values undergird the efforts of all who pretend to science; and, by their efforts, scientists—so far as they are dedicated scientists—declare these values in their daily pursuits. The effects of social scientific research reach beyond this, however, inasmuch as the results of such research strike at the very heart of our ideas about the good life. This occurs, not as a result of advocacy, but by making clear where our choices lead and when our ideals are in conflict. For example, James Coleman's [29] study of the influences of desegregation on school learning has caused many of us to *reconsider* some of our previous notions about community schools. Consequently, we understand somewhat more fully some of the alternatives that are open to us.

If Redfield is correct, then by the very nature of their products, the

---

and Jack R. Fraenkel (Scranton, Pa.: International Textbook Company, 1969), p. 19.
[27] *Ibid.*, p. 20.
[28] *Ibid.*, p. 21.
[29] James A. Coleman, *Equality of Educational Opportunity* (Washington, D.C.: U.S. Department of Health, Education and Welfare, 1966).

social sciences force us into making value choices. They push us to the brink, if not over the brink—into the realm of deciding what *ought* to be done by *influencing* the values we hold. But the question before us can be stated: "Does science dictate oughts?" or, "Can an *ought* be logically inferred from an *is* of science?"

Let us examine this matter further by turning to the enterprise of education. Let us note its dual nature. In the first place, education can be studied scientifically. In fact, as we have already seen in the first part of this chapter, efforts have been made to construct scientific theories for teaching. But these theories appear to lack the explanatory and predictive powers of certain theories in the physical sciences.

In the second place, education is a practical enterprise. Decisions constantly must be made about what should be done—for example, about what ought to be taught and how it ought to be taught. Since science does not deal with the *ought* in its research (even though the results of science bear upon *ought* decisions) and since our research in education has not produced very conclusive results, educators have continued to draw upon a second-order theory. This is the speculative theory which we referred to earlier. Some call it philosophy of education. It usually advances a set of excellences and practices for education that may be supported by some scientific evidence; but, to a very large extent, appeal is made to some kinds of metaphysical presuppositions.

One of the most influential pieces of speculative theory in education has been Rousseau's *Emile*.[30] Even as late as 1915, when John and Evelyn Dewey published their description of progressive schools, they remarked that a majority of the schools had been rather obviously and extensively influenced by Rousseau's theory of education, most particularly at the point of concern for the learner.

Rousseau began his *Emile* with the ontological presupposition that all things are good as they come from the hand of God, but man meddles with them and they become corrupt. And so it is with the education of children. Man rushes into educating his young, who are made worse by his efforts. Instead, we should understand that children

---

[30] Jean Jacques Rousseau, *Emile* (London: J. M. Brent and Sons Ltd., 1911).

are taught by what Rousseau called three masters: things, adults, and nature. Since the third of these—that is, the organs and faculties of the child—is the only master that cannot be controlled, it should dominate. From this follows the most important rule of education, "Do not save time but lose it." What Rousseau meant by this was that between the time of birth and age twelve the pupil passed through the "most dangerous period of his life" and that considerable care should be taken not to teach him things which he did not need to know or that he could not understand. It was the time when "errors and vices spring up, while as yet there is no means to destroy them," for the organs and faculties had not time to adequately mature. Rousseau believed that by the time the means of destruction were ready, the roots would have gone too deep to be pulled up. Thus, rather than force the child into learning, we should try to teach the child what is of use to him. This, we will find, will take all our time.

> Why urge him to the studies of an age he may never reach, to the neglect of those studies which meet his present needs? . . . A child knows he must become a man; all the ideas he may have as to man's estates are so many opportunities for his instruction, but he should remain in complete ignorance of those ideas which are beyond his grasp. My whole book is one continued argument in support of this fundamental principle of education.

At this juncture it should be carefully observed that Rousseau was attempting to infer from an ontological statement about the nature of man how education should be conducted. As a number of persons have attempted to show, a move from an ontological presupposition to what *ought* to be done, is fraught with danger. If one chooses this theoretical route—and many still do, perhaps more out of necessity than out of desire, because of the limitations of our scientific evidence in education—he is immediately faced with two predicaments. In the first place, there are conflicting notions concerning the nature of man. It is said that man is a naked ape, that he is a rational and social animal, that he is good, that he is bad, that he is neither good nor bad but simply a product of his environment. Not all these can be true, for, in fact, some are contradictory. It is a fundamental rule of logic that a thing cannot both be true and not true at the same time. Thus, how can it be true that man is both *only* good and *only* bad at the same time?

Another difficulty is encountered when we try to work out ends and means for education from presuppositions about the nature of man. Nothing *necessarily* follows, in the logical sense of *necessary,* from such presuppositions. Man is a rational animal, or so some claim. Does it follow from this that we should teach him trigonometry, biochemistry, music, art, or social studies, or conventional chronological history? Ought we to indoctrinate him to believe in the superiority of a particular way of life or restrict ourselves to teaching only such facts as that frogs lay eggs and bitches give birth to their pups? As Sidney Hook [31] put it, to know the nature of the egg does not tell you whether you *ought* to scramble, fry, set, or throw it. Yet persons continue to pretend that they draw necessary inferences about what *ought* to be done from such presuppositions. Even Dewey appears to have been caught up on this when he maintained that one must first get his concept of experience clear before he can think about education. But his Pedagogic Creed,[32] containing the seed of nearly every idea he had about education, appeared about thirty years before he wrote *Experience and Nature*.[33]

Hopefully, the present discussion has helped us to see that *oughts do not necessarily follow* from scientific generalizations any more than they do from metaphysical propositions.

Deductive logic is a system of thinking governed by certain rules. A basic rule of this system is that no term can appear in a conclusion that does not appear in one of the premises of the argument. But this rule is violated when we attempt to infer *oughts* from either ontological or strict empirical premises. As David Hume [34] noted a long time ago, the *ought* is smuggled, often undetected, into our conclusion without it appearing in any of our empirical premises. Perhaps an illustration will make this clear. In the conclusion to a report to a

---

[31] Sidney Hook, *Education for Modern Man: A New Perspective* (New York: Alfred A. Knopf, 1963). See Chapter Three for his discussion of inference.

[32] John Dewey, "My Pedagogic Creed," *The School Journal,* Vol. 54, No. 3 (January 16, 1897), pp. 77–80.

[33] John Dewey, *Experience and Nature* (New York: Dover Publications, Inc., 1958).

[34] David Hume, *Treatise on Human Nature,* Book III, Part I, Section V. For a somewhat different viewpoint, see Stephen C. Pepper, *The Sources of Value* (Berkeley, Calif.: University of California Press, 1958).

foundation, two authors claim that several "empirically verified conclusions" were judged to be significant. Among these was the conclusion that "Evaluation *should* [our emphasis] be an integral and important part of any new teacher education curriculum." It is obvious that these authors believe *oughts* flow logically from empirical findings.

How then shall we answer our question, "Can theory guide practice?" First, we shall want to remember that in deciding what ought to be done, we cannot move without logical difficulties of the sorts we have been discussing. But, at the same time, we do not want to say that in making *ought* determinations theory is useless. That would be tantamount to declaring our knowledge useless. We would be left saying that one person's opinion is just as good as the next, that the ignoramus is just as qualified as the informed person to make *ought* determinations.

But this can be shown, at least in some cases, to be an odd stance. Take, for example, the case of whether one ought to continue smoking. One would prefer, it would seem, the opinion of a medical expert to that of a barber who knows next to nothing about medicine. Or, take another example. Ought mothers to place pictures and erect mobiles in nurseries? This would seem to be a matter to which those with the most reliable information could speak with some authority. Certainly the opinion of the child psychologist must be thought of as more pertinent in this instance than that of the carpenter who has fathered no children and who had had neither the opportunity nor the inclination to study them. Likewise, the well-educated man might have something more important to say about what ought to be sought for by way of the ends of education than the ignoramus. If this is not the case, then it would seem odd to try to justify the advancement of knowledge on any other grounds than the pleasure that is afforded by its collection.

If social science theory has the impact Redfield suggested and if theory is useful in making decisions about what ought to be done, as we have tried to show, then we can use the results of science to support our decisions about teaching. However, we cannot prove them true or false by appeal to either metaphysical or empirical premises. Rather than alarm us, the knowledge that the aims and means of education cannot be necessarily inferred from either scientific propositions or from metaphysical presuppositions, should spare us from the looseness and dogmatism that have so often characterized our theories for teaching.

2 | From Theories for Learning to Theories for Teaching

**B. CLAUDE MATHIS and
WILLIAM C. McGAGHIE**

In our endeavor to understand reality we are somewhat like a man trying to understand the mechanism of a closed watch. He sees the face and the moving hands, even hears its ticking, but he has no way of opening the case. If he is ingenious he may form some picture of a mechanism which could be responsible for all the things he observes, but he may never be quite sure his picture is the only one which could explain his observations. He will never be able to compare his picture with the real mechanism and he cannot even imagine the possibility or the meaning of such a comparison. But he certainly believes that, as his knowledge increases, his picture of reality will become simpler and simpler and will explain a wider and wider range of his sensuous impressions.[1]

By using a metaphor for his definition of theory Einstein shows more than his personal genius. In a roundabout way he tells us theories have a purpose. They stimulate and guide our thinking as we try to explain the world as we see it. He also tells us theories are things that *we* create—they are inventions, not discoveries. Men use theories to help find out how their world is constructed, how it operates, and, in some instances, how it can be changed. Seen in this light, theories are helpful tools when it comes to organizing our thoughts before putting them to work. Moreover, the simplest theory is often the best theory. Einstein's Theory of Relativity is stated in the equation

---

[1] Albert Einstein and Leopold Infeld, *The Evolution of Physics* (New York: Simon and Schuster, 1938), p. 31.

$E = mc^2$, a masterpiece of simplicity and summative excellence. Still, it is man-made and unless we believe Einstein had access to sources of information apart from the world of men, we must submit his creation to constant cross-examination, as well as treating it with the respect it demands.

What Theories Are

For the purposes of this chapter, we should like to define theories as systems of statements arranged in a hierarchical pattern according to rules of logic, that offer a structural framework for empirical investigation. Theories provide a conceptual frame-of-reference for persons who seek to organize the seemingly random events that nature produces. Theories give direction to research workers since their complex networks of conceptual relationships must be thoroughly tested before the theoretical architecture can be accepted as valid or rejected as inadequate. They encourage the scientist to pursue his experiments by giving him tentative boundaries within which his results may be interpreted. Theoretical *validity* is the aim of persons who assume responsibility for testing natural conditions—validity being the verification of the "truth," logic, and lawful nature of the theoretical structure.

The notion of lawfulness connotes another set of requirements which bear directly upon theoretical principles. Lawful relations amid a theoretical structure imply that, given the appropriate set of conditions, the introduction of event A will consistently result in a concomitant change in event B. Central to this position is the consistency of the relations between A and B. These relations must occur with a high degree of reliability, unaffected by the passage of time, before a theory is acceptable. Thus the statutory elements within a validated theoretical framework must also possess a high degree of *vitality* to strengthen the position of that framework as a worthwhile tool for scientific investigation.

Social Science Theories

Social scientists deal with theory on a regular basis. They attempt to construct theoretical frameworks to better understand and perhaps predict the complex relationships associated with human behavior.

With a limited degree of success, social scientists have been able to demonstrate contiguity between phenomena to a degree where their lawfulness is unquestioned. Thorndike's Law of Effect in psychology and the Law of Supply and Demand in economics are examples which posit specified relations among theoretical entities, given appropriate conditions. The predictability of human behavior when the necessary reward or production-distribution circumstances are in force has been validated consistently by numerous social scientists. We may assert that psychological theory and economic theory have profited considerably from these statements of lawful relations, and to this day the laws of effect and supply and demand are considered fundamental to their respective disciplines.

Educators are not so fortunate. Those of us who deal with teaching and learning recognize the issues are so complex that any attempt to construct a theoretical framework for their integration may be hazardous. One major problem is that teaching and learning have traditionally been studied in the area of education as if they were separate processes. Teaching is usually treated in the literature of education as if it is concerned only with the activities of a teacher or some technological surrogate which attempts to alter the behavior of the learner. Learning is held to be *a relatively permanent change in behavior resulting from experience*,[2] and has usually been investigated as a process which involves only the learner. Another difficulty in the study of teaching and learning is that while learning (in terms of observable behavior change) is explicit, the concept of teaching is not at all clear and tends to be elusive when subjected to attempts at conceptualization. As a result, a theory for teaching, though closely allied to a parent theory of learning, represents a partially dependent though considerably broader conceptual scheme. United, theories for teaching and learning define education in a context which joins the teacher and the learner as parts of a process, adding social dimensions to formerly discrete events.[3]

[2] B. Claude Mathis, John W. Cotton, and Lee Sechrest, *Psychological Foundations of Education* (New York: Academic Press, 1970), p. 48.

[3] Throughout the remainder of this chapter, the term "theory for teaching" will be used to refer to an educational process which defines teaching as essentially a didactic event including both teacher and learner in an interdependent relationship.

Education refers to a process that occurs among persons—typically, a teacher and students. It is the teacher's responsibility to provide for change among students—to teach them—so that students are somehow different when their association with the teacher is ended. But unlike other sciences, in which precise control of conditions may lead to insight concerning lawful relations, education must account for a constellation of variables which influence teaching and learning simultaneously.

Theory Building About Teaching

To gain an approximation to the precision that theory building about teaching demands, educators usually borrow insights about the human process from other social and behavioral sciences, incorporating them in an eclectic framework. Principles of learning (psychology); roles, status, power (sociology); customs (anthropology); distribution of goods and services (economics); and maturation and development (biology) quickly come to mind. The effects of these variables on teaching and learning are formidable when taken singly. Together, their effects can be baffling. The interaction of these disciplinary sources for the validation of a theory for teaching makes it difficult for any one scholar or any one discipline to conceptualize the task of developing such a theory. We also have reason to believe that the vitality of theory building in education is jeopardized by our rapidly changing social system. The ultimate goal of theoretical formulation is to demonstrate lawful relations among variables of interest. Furthermore, as demonstrations of these lawful relations accumulate, they usually act as precedents for further theory construction. But *un*precedented conditions—those not foreseen at the time of initial theoretical development—may negate the basic principles and assumptions that have guided preliminary theorizing. A rapidly changing social and technological climate may enforce a time dependence upon a theory of teaching/learning, thus endangering both validity and vitality.

A recent statement on theory building under the rubric of instruction contains a definition and a list of components which can guide attempts at instructional theory formulation. (It is noteworthy that these comments are related to "instruction," which is only one of the many terms used to define teaching. An expansion of the concept of teaching including a discussion of its numerous possible definitions is given by Green.)[4] First, a definition of instruction:

> ... a theory of instruction consists of a set of propositions stating relationships between, on the one hand, measures of the outcomes of education, and on the other hand, measures of both the conditions to which the learner is exposed and the variables representing characteristics of the learner.[5]

Components associated with an adequate theory of instruction are direct descendants of this definition:

1. ... [An] empirical base [will be necessary]—the propositions of the theory must have a clear relation to data.
2. A theory of instruction will have to represent the relationship between a wide range of learning conditions and achievements.
3. The optimum conditions would be those which maximized some function, say a linear function, of the measures of the variables defining the outcomes.
4. A theory of instruction of any value will have to be based on quantitative data, but these data will probably be reducible to a set of verbal nonmathematical propositions.[6]

These comments are intended to reinforce the idea that the architecture of a theory for teaching must be comprehensive and harmonious. Yet the relationships between behavioral outcomes and the conditions under which learning occurs are too often too vague and elusive for even the most sophisticated experimental methodology. The criteria cited above demand greater clarity. They require that theories of education be built according to exacting specifications so that the relationships between relevant antecedent conditions (teaching) and consequent behavioral outcomes (learning) can be identified,

---

[4] Thomas F. Green, "A Topology of the Teaching Concept," *Studies in Philosophy and Education,* Vol. 3 (Winter, 1964–65), pp. 284–319.
[5] Robert M. W. Travers, "Towards Taking the Fun out of Building a Theory of Instruction," *Teachers College Record,* Vol. 68 (1966), pp. 49–60.
[6] *Ibid.*

understood, controlled, and ultimately predicted. Furthermore, the reducibility of empirical data to simple conceptual propositions is necessary so that a wide audience (i.e., teachers in any context) can employ a theory for teaching for the welfare of their students.

Psychological Perspectives for Teaching Theories

Because of our training as psychologists and our attempts to apply this training to education, our entrance into the complexities of teaching theory is through the perspective of psychology. The points of view about learning which have appeared in the literature of psychology are indeed a central consideration for a theory for teaching. With respect to our training, however, we must advise the reader that, while we tend to be actuarial (i.e., we usually require empirical substantiation for points of view about psychological phenomena), we cannot deny that at this time the issues of human learning and the teaching designed to promote it often defy the logician's grasp. Reason, data, and experience are too often inconsistent. Consequently, as we discuss some differing outlooks of learning, the reader must be wary that this reflective exercise is not meant to be evaluative. Each perspective has costs and benefits that must be weighed according to the situational constraints that will directly influence any theory for teaching when it is applied.

Key Conceptions about Human Learning

Within the science of psychology there are differing points of view concerning the fundamental assumptions about human learning. This disagreement on fundamentals (e.g., the basic nature of man including drives, perception, motives, and values) has resulted in the emergence of different "schools" of psychology. One's advocacy of the perspective associated with one of these subdivisions acts to color his perception, interpretation, and action as he tries to make sense of human behavior. In teaching, it is especially important to recognize that the behavior of both the teacher and student(s) must be accounted for in order for a theory for teaching to be worthwhile. Thus, for any school of psychology to be an effective starting point in an effort to build a theory for teaching, its basic assumptions must explain the social aspects of the classroom, in addition to the character of the individual participants.

It becomes important then to explore some of the more popular schools of psychology to determine if their implicit assumptions on how humans learn can provide recommendations for teaching. Since these schools of thought are broad in scope, it is necessary to advise the reader that this brief scenario sketches only the outlines of these systems. The origins [7] and principal assumptions [8] of each of these schools of psychological thought have been dealt with elsewhere and it is our purpose to provide only a capsule description of those having the most substantial following. A more careful examination may reveal points of convergence among them. Indeed, the most fruitful approach would be to search for their interactions and common reference points while using their insights on learning to gain insights for teaching. Unfortunately, integrative interpretations of learning are only beginning to emerge in psychology. Each system discussed below thus has an empirical base which suggests teaching strategies consistent with the logic of its point of view. It should be pointed out, moreover, that integrative, or eclectic, strategies are speculative at best. The development of integrative theory from the social and behavioral sciences represents the next step in the maturation of understanding human behavior.

Behaviorism

B. F. Skinner is the major contemporary spokesman for behaviorism. The Skinnerian perspective is based on what is called the *functional analysis of behavior,* a methodology that attempts to isolate the "contingencies of reinforcement" which shape and maintain behavior.[9]

---

[7] David L. Krantz, ed., *Schools of Psychology* (New York: Appleton-Century-Crofts, 1969).
[8] Gordon W. Allport, "Psychological Models for Guidance," *Harvard Educational Review,* Vol. 32 (1962), pp. 373–381.
[9] Skinner's behavioristic approach to learning represents an extension and

Reinforcement contingencies are links between behavioral responses and their effects. The study of reinforcement contingencies attempts to demonstrate that behavior is a function of its consequences.[10] Another significant influence on human behavior is the past occurrence of reinforcement. Behaviorists assert that responses which have been strengthened in the past have a higher probability of being emitted again than responses which have not been strengthened.[11] It is a combination of the ambient contingencies of reinforcement coupled with a past history of reinforcement which determines the nature and direction of an individual's behavior. Indeed, determinism is the *sine qua non* of the behavioral school of psychology. The functional analysis of behavior proposes to uncover the forces that determine how an individual will behave.

The foremost assumption which underlies B. F. Skinner's analysis of behavior is that behavior is controlled by environmental contingencies of reinforcement. Sources of reinforcement *external* to man determine his behavior. Thus a coed's ability to socialize with young men is often determined by whether or not she receives requests for dates. Her dating behavior is controlled by events she is unable to embrace (figuratively, that is). The environment that controls

---

further elaboration of the point of view first advanced by E. L. Thorndike in the Law of Effect, which defined a reward in terms of the effect of a response. A further elaboration of Skinner's position as it applies to teaching can be found in B. F. Skinner, *The Technology of Teaching* (New York: Appleton-Century-Crofts, 1968).

[10] This defines what Skinner has chosen to call operant behavior. Another form of behavior of concern to the Skinnerian school is respondent (reflexive) behavior, in which responses are a function of their antecedent stimuli. The operant model more closely resembles the type of learning that occurs in schools, so our discussion of behaviorism will focus on the operant side of Skinner's behavior theory.

[11] In this section the terms "reinforcement" and "response strengthening" are synonymous. The reader should also be aware that reinforcement has variable forms: (a) positive, which strengthens responses by the contingent presentation of "rewarding" events; and (b) negative, which strengthens responses with the contingent removal of "aversive" events. Response-contingent neutral events will eventually cause responding to extinguish (die out). Behavior may be suppressed with punishment. None of these cases requires that the person responding engage in wilful mediation of psychological processes.

behavior—namely, those men to whom the coed has access—is basic in this case. In other cases, the controlling environmental contingencies are less obvious: the cloistered monk, the martyr, and the dedicated teacher, to name a few. Yet according to a behavioral purist, the behavior of each is still generated and maintained by the environment in which he resides. Ostensibly, prayer is strengthened by God, martyrdom by the prospect of sainthood, and dedicated teaching by a paycheck and possibly satisfaction in promoting learning among students.

Teachers who accept the behavioral perspective must assume the behavior of students is controlled by their past and present environment. An additional intuitive step leads to the conclusion that the environment in which teacher meets students—the classroom—is filled with possible reinforcement contingencies that can influence learning. The antics of a classroom clown are reinforced by attention from his peers so he "learns" to be more disruptive; a withdrawn student "learns" that his environment does not serve up reinforcement for gregariousness, resulting in the strengthening of silence; a productive student "learns" solid geometry because the teacher smiles, gives him an A, and Dad lends him the car. The environment that controls behavior is complex; pervasive; and, to the untrained eye, random.

Recognizing these possibilities, a behaviorally oriented teacher sets out to structure an environment whose contingencies of reinforcement strengthen the behavior he considers appropriate. The task becomes one of constructing a classroom where the probability that students will be reinforced for emitting learning behavior is maximized. Definitions of appropriate learning are situational, being affected by the teacher's philosophy, the community in which the school is located, and perhaps the educational *Zeitgeist*. The point is that the teacher (who is an important part of the environment, incidentally) is in a position to control student behavior by manipulating contingencies of reinforcement so that the randomness that typifies many classrooms is eliminated. Such a teacher is not willing to assume his students will learn by chance. Instead, he carefully prepares a blueprint for student learning according to the principles of behaviorism. Michael has outlined some of the principles of effective usage of behaviorism for educators.

1. Consequence Identification
    Reinforcers and punishers must ultimately be identified as such in terms of their effects on the behavior of the learner.
2. Automaticity
    Consequences affect behavior in an automatic or mechanistic way. It is not necessary that the learner be able to verbalize about the relation between his behavior and the consequences, or even verbalize that the consequence has occurred.
3. Relevant Criteria
    When the main use of reinforcement and punishment is educational accomplishment, these consequences should be closely linked to the criteria of accomplishment.
4. Consistency
    The teacher must attend to the consequences of the learner's behavior at all times and in all situations.
5. Immediacy
    Consequences should be as close in time as possible to the behavior responsible for them.
6. Frequency
    Optimal reinforcement frequency is usually underestimated.
7. Small Steps
    When an educational unit of work is too large to permit an optimally high frequency of reinforcement it should be broken into smaller steps.
8. Unplanned Punishment Effects
    The total effect of reinforcement which requires prior worsening [deprivation] includes the punishment effects of the worsening.
9. Effective Contracting
    When consequence arrangement takes the form of a contract between the teacher and the learner, the contract should be (a) clear, (b) fair, and (c) honest.[12]

These principles emphasize how a behavioral teacher controls his students through a carefully arranged environment so that the learn-

[12] From Jack Michael, *Management of Behavioral Consequences in Education*, Southwest Regional Laboratory for Educational Research and Development (1967); reprinted in Roger Ulrich, Thomas Stachnik, and John Mabry, eds., *Control of Human Behavior*, Vol. II (Glenview, Ill.: Scott, Foresman and Co., 1970), pp. 28–35.

ing which occurs cannot be attributed to good fortune or the phases of the moon. To the contrary, learning is attributed to the craftsmanship of the teacher as he engineers an environment whose effects on learning are direct, observable, and precise.

Placing emphasis on the importance of the environment to control student learning, behaviorism does not consider motives to be intrinsic to an individual. Motivation is the result of events occurring outside the skin and is not thought to arise from an individual's idiosyncratic needs. A person learns to be a thief, an artist, or whatever, depending on whether his environment has strengthened thievery or aesthetics in the past and maintains such behavior at present.[13] Values cannot be ascribed to a person but emerge from the milieu in which he behaves. A salesman values a fat contract because his selling behavior is strengthened by a promotion. A teacher may value classroom silence, perfect punctuation, and deference from students because they are presumably associated with learning. In each situation the environment is the supreme court of appeal—motives and values are independent of individuals.

When behaviorists search for the causes of behavior they have become fond of saying "the subject is always right," meaning the subject is merely reacting to the contingencies of reinforcement that affect him. To modify behavior, all one has to do is rearrange the external consequence structure to make it contingent upon desired responses. Cast in this light a teacher "creates" his students by motivating learning through reinforcement; students value learning when it leads to demonstrable payoffs. In either case student behavior is determined by the controlling forces in the classroom. Responsibility for behavior lies apart from students themselves.

Psychoanalytic

The psychoanalytic school of thought finds its roots in the teachings of Sigmund Freud. Although Freud was not a learning theorist, the scientific study of personality in psychology has had as its major

---

[13] A recent article by Skinner presents a behavioral analysis of the development of a poet. See B. F. Skinner, "On 'Having' a Poem," *Saturday Review*, Vol. 55, No. 29 (July 15, 1972), pp. 32–35.

historical influence the theoretical formulations of Freud and his followers. The experimental study of personality provides important data for those psychologists who study learning as a process in which motivation, interest, values, and attitudes are central in determining behavior. Freud's work represents one of the first attempts to move from the philosophical to the scientific domain in order to explain human behavior. His psychoanalytic theory is an outgrowth of his training as a physician and his attempt to cure nervous disorders by "talking them out"—a procedure designed to help neurotic patients recover by searching for causes believed to be buried in their pasts. After success in private practice Freud began to write about his new technique and quickly gained prominence, as well as a considerable following in European medical circles. A series of lectures at Clark University at the turn of the century provided a forum where Freud's beliefs about human behavior could be exported to the United States. From that time he gained a reputation in the United States as a brilliant clinician and scholar. His impact on psychological thinking—particularly on the development of personality theory—has been pervasive.[14]

It is important to point out that Freud developed his psychoanalytic theory from experience in the clinic, not in the laboratory. His propositions concerning the etiology and manifestation of human behavior are a result of his insights in treating behavior problems with his "talking cure," a medical background, and the naturalistic scientific tradition which prevailed in nineteenth-century Vienna. Thus, while Freud is held to be one of the most influential social scientists of this century, his approach to the study of human behavior was not scientific in an experimental sense. His hypotheses often cannot be tested according to established procedure, but seek validation through observation and personal interpretation. This reliance on subjective insight is of highest priority for both understanding and applying psychoanalytic theory.

Psychoanalytic theory, as behaviorism, is based on a principle of

---

[14] The interested reader may find an expanded version of Freudian theory in Calvin Hall and Gardner Lindzey, *Theories of Personality* (New York: John Wiley and Sons, 1957), pp. 29–75.

determinism. But unlike behaviorism, this theory does not accept the notion that forces external to an individual exert control over his behavior. Freudians believe the origins of human behavior exist within the individual himself, that *biologically* oriented impulses are responsible for the direction and intensity of behavior.[15] Unless a person is able to gain insight about these root causes of behavior, therefore becoming able to anticipate and control their effects, he will be subject to internal influences that he is unable to regulate. Similar to behaviorism, psychoanalytic theory holds that the individual is not fully in control of his behavior. On gaining insight into the causes of his behavior, however, he is in a position to assume greater degrees of self-control and, consequently, personal responsibility.

In addition to biological determinism, psychoanalytic theory, as Freud developed it, places major emphasis on life history as a crucial factor in human behavior. While maturing physically, each individual must progress through a series of corollary psychosexual development stages. The stages range from birth[16] to adulthood, each being a significant contributor to an evolving personality structure. The term "psychosexual" is used because progression through each stage involves the resolution of a sexual conflict.[17] Before proceeding to successive levels of development, persons must learn to subdue the pleasure-seeking urges associated with their biological constitution as expectations for self-control arise from society. Take toilet training.

---

[15] Those who have followed Freud in the development of psychoanalytic theory have tended to modify his emphasis on a biological determinism as the basic motive force for behavior. Such scholars as Erich Fromm have helped to redirect psychoanalytic thinking by emphasizing the deterministic effects of culture and society on behavior. Unlike behaviorism, however, neo-Freudian determinism is important only as its effects are internalized by the individual and represented as feelings and attitudes he has about himself and others.

[16] Purists will dispute this point, arguing that psychosexual development begins *in utero*.

[17] In this context, "sexual" is synonyous with "pleasurable." The psychoanalytic school contends that such behavior as eating and evacuation are "sexual" in nature since they provide pleasurable sensations. Neo-Freudian theory tends to emphasize social and interpersonal conflict as a major motivational source. In this context, sexual conflict becomes only one instance in the larger scheme of psychosocial development.

After a year or so most children are trained to control their bowels and bladder. Parental rules are enforced to keep a child's personal satisfaction from becoming "antisocial movements." Control over such impulses is said to develop during the anal stage. By passing through the psychosexual stages in serial order, children and young adults learn to internalize social definitions of appropriate behavior and to compromise their self-centered motives. An unsuccessful progression results in retarded development (i.e., the individual continues to exhibit the traits associated with bygone stages causing arrested [psychological] growth).

Three hypothetical entities account for the struggle between society and the developing person. The *id* represents the primitive urges of man. It is unsocialized and instinctual, operating on the "pleasure principle" as it seeks immediate gratification of impulses. Antagonistic to the id is the *superego,* an agent of social control. The superego represents society as it imposes restrictions upon the pleasure-seeking id. The id and superego are at opposite ends of the pleasure-seeking continuum. Caught between these two opposing forces is the *ego,* which represents the personification of man. Ego must constantly mediate impulses of the id and of the countercontrol based in the superego. Satisfactory development occurs when the ego possesses the strength to hold both id and superego at bay—to balance their opposition. "Ego strength" then, is the psychoanalytic term that describes the favored characteristic of man. Such a man recognizes the existence of his baser passions but seeks their satisfaction in concert with reasonable social restriction. When children have temper tantrums, we assume that id forces are responsible. Students who are always deferent, blindly following even the most absurd rules of conduct, display an exaggerated superego. In either case, if these extreme modes of behavior cannot be compromised, the ego is weakened. An oversupply of tantrums or acquiescence shows that optimal development, in terms of ego strength, is hindered.

In order to translate a psychoanalytic theory of development to a system of propositions that may be titled a theory for teaching, we must recognize that hard-and-fast rules are not available for the revision. Yet operating without a format for theory construction, we are still prepared to present criteria for a theory for teaching consistent with this paradigm :

1. Psychoanalytic theory emphasizes the dynamics of the human process within each person. It demands an idiographic rather than a nomothetic approach. To favor the welfare of student groups is to risk the possible reduction of benefits for individual members.
2. Teachers are pseudo-clinicians. Their major responsibility is to make provisions for the development of ego strength, however defined, among students. Consequently, personality development among students has priority over the academic and intellectual discipline that most schools strive for.
3. Teachers must be aware of the dynamics that have shaped the course of their lives, being able to capitalize on their strengths while attempting to gain greater insight into possible sources of personal weakness. Bettelheim writes : "For the teacher, this would mean regaining her own repressed childhood memories, her reaching a better understanding of what shaped her in her own infancy and childhood, just as all children are shaped. Only then could she educate children in a way that was neither a repressive molding of the young nor an acting out on them of old fears and resentments." [18]

A psychoanalytic teacher is constantly vigilant in his attempts to foster ego strength in his students and himself. He has faith in the developmental potential of the human species. He realizes that *assisting* students to resolve their academic and personal dilemmas is the chief teaching function. He is nonauthoritarian, nondogmatic, and sensitive to the subjective meanings associated with human behavior. Another passage from Bettelheim further clarifies the psychoanalytic approach : "The difference between an education that is informed by psychoanalysis and one that we might call a reactionary, authoritarian education is that the first one considers seriously the inner meanings of an outward-directed behavior. The second counts only the achieve-

---

[18] Bruno Bettelheim, "Psychoanalysis and Education," *The School Review*, Vol. 77 (1969), p. 74.

ment, and never mind its inner meaning or its cost to the total personality." [19]

What can we state as functional prerequisites for a psychoanalytic theory for teaching? To begin with, the framework calls for an orientation that eliminates prescriptive teaching directed solely toward academic achievement at the expense of personality development. This is not to say that achievement is unimportant, only that the long-term welfare of students is based in ego strength rather than knowledge. Another point is the assumption that values emerge from the social milieu, whereas motives are buried within each person. If left unchecked by superego control, asocial id forces are likely to result in motivation that is socially deleterious. Persons must learn to internalize social sanctions while satisfying their biological needs. This is the ego's job—a balancing act that occurs in all developing persons. Teachers can aid in ego-strength development by helping students recognize and perhaps compromise their singular wants with social regulations. Finally, the teacher must be fully aware of his own ego strength. He must possess self-insight in order to understand human personality dynamics, while helping his students become satisfied, yet responsible, persons.

Humanistic

While the behavioral school of thought believes that "man is what you make him," and the psychoanalytic approach in essence views him as a creature with a basic capacity for behaving impulsively (i.e., unless id forces and superego demands are effectively compromised by the development of a rational and socially rewarding ego structure), the humanistic perspective carries a more positive connotation of the nature of man. Humanistic psychologists perceive man to be basically a loving animal. This stance is quite different from the vision of man as a malleable creature who is subject to shaping, or as a potentially self-seeking organism. Personified, humanistic man is one who is

[19] *Ibid.* This passage points out the largest difference between the behaviorist and the psychoanalytic schools of psychology. Behaviorists do not necessarily attribute meaning or subjective interpretation to classroom learning. The psychoanalytic school, on the other hand, insists that ego strength develops only through individual mediation of experience (the classroom being no exception).

constantly striving for actualization of the self. He is searching for the fullest possible realization of his potentialities in the here and now. He is neither subject to the determination of incapacitating childhood experience nor a victim of a reinforcement history based on external control. This man is existential. He lives in and exists for the present moment, attempting to maximize his human potential and to realize his highest personal capabilities.

Humanists assert that man is motivated by growth. Freed from external and historical constraints, his potential to grow as a loving, productive, functional person is manifested. The *process of becoming* rather than a specifically defined goal is the ultimate objective. Such a man is not static; his optimal growth is dependent upon constant personal experience directed toward self-actualization.[20] Since he is a member of the human species, though, man is subject to all the attendant frailties and uncertainties of character. Biological motives have some influence on his behavior. Drives related to hunger, thirst, protection, and sex demand satisfaction. But once sated, the lower-order and pleasure-seeking drives are no longer paramount in his hierarchy of concern and behavior. He is then freed to pursue the higher-order human needs which separate man from lower organisms, to wit: love, aesthetics, productivity, and so on.

Humanists consider self-actualized man to be unrestrained. He is free to make personal decisions regarding personal goals, and to direct himself toward personal self-fulfillment. Central to this doctrine is the importance of the choices an individual must make for himself during the course of his life. It is at these critical choice-points that a potential for anxiety and crisis emerges. One's ability to make personally and socially responsible decisions at critical moments is a necessary requirement for self-actualization. The ability to fulfil one's own human needs on one's own human terms throughout life is a fundamental characteristic of a self-actualized person.

Extrapolated to teaching, the humanistic approach focuses on the quality of the interpersonal relationship that exists between teacher and learner. Indeed, the title of teacher is considered inappropriate. Carl Rogers, the major spokesman for humanism, has coined the term

[20] It is unclear whether this growth is ideally linear or of another order.

"facilitator" to replace "teacher." That is, teachers must become facilitators of learning.

It is the facilitator's role to constantly direct his energies toward the development of genuine interpersonal relationships between himself and the learner. In this way he makes provisions for learning in the most human sense. The facilitator must be honest as he relates to the student. He must be completely open with his whole self. He must exhibit his human strengths and weaknesses in a way that reveals his unmet potentialities. Encouraging the student to do the same without passing judgment or centering on his shortcomings creates an atmosphere in which significant experiential learning, unbridled by characteristic fear and hesitancy, can occur. The current movement toward so-called free schools rests upon the virtues of humanistic teaching. Students are free to pursue their own interests, without interference, under a protective umbrella of interpersonal warmth. Free schools facilitate learning through experience in being human rather than coercion.

Humanistic teaching is intended to create a situation in which reciprocal prizing, altruism, and recognition can replace the usual stratified roles that traditional teaching requires. Learning must become a partnership in experience in which each individual is worthy of the other's trust. The facilitator must be prepared to take extreme risks in terms of the traditional teaching role. No longer prescribing role-appropriate behavior or learning requirements, he must be oriented completely toward the actualization potential of his students. He facilitates as a human being quite apart from his position in the age, institutional, or hierarchical structure. Thus having torn down the usual interpersonal façade, the student and facilitator are free to share their positive human qualities. The result is an empathic mutual understanding based on trust and love.

Implicit in humanistic teaching is the understanding that the student has the option to reject the facilitator's offerings since only the student is fully equipped to define his own needs and aspirations. Further, it is held that the substance of what is presented is not necessarily that which is learned—or should be. Contemporary social, political, and technological change is occurring at a pace that almost defies our conceptual grasp. By focusing on substance educators imply that the environment is static, predictable. Yet in a changing world we cannot depend on substance to provide security. Only the process of seeking knowledge, the why's and how's of the search itself, are truly relevant to citizens of the future. Facilitators must avoid the possibility that students consider them a factual repository because the future will demand new skills and offer totally new possibilities for actualization.

A statement by Rogers summarizes the humanistic perspective on learning:

> Let me define . . . the elements which are involved in such significant or experiential learning. *It has a quality of personal involvement*—the whole person in both his feeling and cognitive aspects being in the learning event. *It is self-initiated.* Even when the impetus or stimulus comes from the outside, the sense of discovery, of reaching out, of grasping and comprehending, comes from within. *It is pervasive.* It makes a difference in the behavior, the attitudes, perhaps even the personality of the learner. *It is evaluated by the learner.* He knows whether it is meeting his need, whether it leads toward what he *wants* to know, whether it illuminates the dark area of ignorance he is experiencing. The locus of evaluation, we might say, resides definitely in the learner. *Its essence is meaning.* When such learning takes place, the element of meaning to the learner is built into the whole experience.[21]

Implications of Psychological Theories

Having reviewed the behaviorist, psychoanalytic, and humanistic theories in relation to learning, it is clear that their underlying assumptions lead to opposing theories for teaching. Definitions of learning and teaching are different in each case. The locus of control, sources of motivation, value judgments, and optimal educational outcomes are at variance. Even the methods used to validate a theory for teaching will be different: behaviorists demand "effectiveness" as symbolized by the smooth gradient of a mathematical curve, placing little faith in human inference; psychoanalysts rely on the student's personal insight and the possible development of ego strength when the classroom

---

[21] Carl R. Rogers, *Freedom to Learn* (Columbus, Ohio: Charles E. Merrill Publishing Co., 1969), p. 5.

becomes a therapeutic enclosure; humanists opt for student testimonial that, indeed, growth toward reaching the highest levels of learning and interpersonal potential is occurring. By unconditionally accepting any of these three outlooks, a theory builder aligns his vision concerning the purposes of education and the proper activities of teachers and students to satisfy them.

A theory for teaching then, is dependent upon a theoretician's perception of the learning and teaching he attempts to interpret. Given a "slow learner," each theory explains the problem differently. This student is the product of an environment that does not reinforce learning in a systematic way. To improve the child, change his learning environment (behaviorist). The student is deficient in ego strength, probably because of past events which inhibit his present development. Provide opportunities for him to restructure his personality so that he will gain insight into the causes of the problem (psychoanalytic). He is "turned off" by learning because of the impersonal, judgmental nature of the school experience. Understanding and empathy must be given unconditionally. Only then will a teacher be able to facilitate meaningful learning (humanistic). In each situation, the student is seen differently and different dimensions of teacher amelioration are called for—even the desirable outcomes of education are inconsistent. *The propositions of each theory of learning result in contrasting theories for teaching.* Each may possess validity and vitality on its own terms, but extrapolation beyond their singular theoretical frameworks leads to interpretive danger.

The task of formulating a theory for teaching based upon a theory of learning must for the present be a tentative exercise. The belief that any individual outlook is authoritative, given the complex nature of educational processes, is unwarranted. Theoreticians must remain flexible, accepting or rejecting perspectives on teaching depending on situational influences regarding the personal needs of their students and the requirements of the larger society. Balancing individual and social needs has long been the bugbear of teachers and psychologists alike. And recognizing the problem is only the first step in our attempt to solve it.

The contemporary "state-of-the-art" with respect to our understanding of teaching and learning—and our attempts to come to terms with the development of a theory for teaching/learning—suggests that the behavioral sciences, and the professionals who represent them, have arrived at one of the many decision points which characterize the growth of knowledge. Teaching and learning are such complex phenomena that to expect from any one system of behavioral analysis all the answers which a theory for teaching/learning must provide is to anticipate the miraculous. What is now needed is not more of the same. Rather, the behaviorist, the personality theorist, and the humanistic psychologist must join together and with others to discover productive strategies which permit them to contrast and correlate their points of view in the interest of determining the theoretical models for teaching/learning which best accommodate the wide range of individual, social, and situational variation associated with the process of education. Movement among disciplines toward interdisciplinary theory building has been given high priority in many centers of scholarly activity; nevertheless, the temptation to remain in one's own field and associate with one's own professional peers is sufficiently rewarded that uni-dimensional thinking about learning and teaching dominates the literature on the subject. A viable theory for teaching/learning will of necessity await the concentrated and cooperative efforts of scholars in the many disciplines which define the study of education. Excursions into this realm of consensus have occupied the life of the scholar in too few instances. A theory for teaching/learning awaits a reordering of priorities in academia.

3 The Believing in Seeing

HUGH G. PETRIE

Consider:

A squad car screeches to a halt on Chicago's south side. Two overworked, frightened white policemen get out and start trying to break up a group of black teenagers who are lounging around on a sidewalk. In their horsing around, the teenagers have been causing passersby to step into the street to get by and have bumped into several. The youths call the interference of the two police officers more harassment by "The Man." The officers simply see themselves as trying to promote law and order.

A sophomore in a college physics class has just finished studying a chapter on kinetic energy. There is a clear sense in which he understands the chapter: he recalls the formulas; he can do the derivations of the lower level laws from the more basic laws; he understands the relationship between kinetic energy, potential energy, and work; and he can discuss these and related concepts intelligently with his instructor and others knowledgeable in physics. Yet he can make no headway whatsoever on the problems at the end of the chapter.

The students in a teacher-training program rebel against the requirement for a philosophy of education course. They do not see how it could possibly be relevant to their needs. After all, what does a linguistic analysis of teaching have to do with how to handle those kids in an inner-city classroom. The professor is indignant. He is not in the business of providing "recipes" for every narrowly construed practical problem his students may face. His job is to provide a perspective—a way of looking at things in general, which, if properly assimilated, is bound to filter down to the students' everyday concerns.

A novice cook begins to make some bread and in reading the recipe comes to the phrase, "knead flour into the dough until it is elastic." The novice has no clear notion of what this means and so just follows the recipe proportions for flour. The result is disastrous. The experienced cook can "feel" the right consistency and so adds much less flour. Possibly it is a "harder" flour and hence absorbs the liquid more readily, so that the feel is right with less flour. The bread turns out fine.

A person cannot see the rabbit in the following Wittgensteinian example; another will not see the duck.[1]

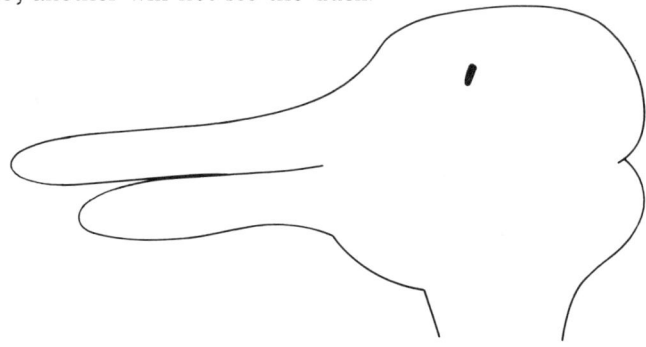

A young middle-class white elementary teacher complains frequently about the black children in his newly integrated classroom. He cannot get them to sit still and learn. They are constantly disrupting the class with their hyperactivity. The teacher's training was at a good college of education in a private university. His student teaching took place at an all-white suburban school. The principal asks a consultant to drop by his classroom and the consultant finds *all* the children to be quite fidgety and active. In addition, the teacher himself seems unable to sit still, yet he only seems to see the activity of the black children.

[1] Ludwig Wittgenstein, *Philosophical Investigation*, G. E. M. Anscombe, 3rd ed. (New York: Macmillan, 1958), p. 194e.

Perceptual Capacities

What do such incredibly diverse situations have in common? I believe they are all examples of an extremely important, but often overlooked, feature of teacher-learning situations—namely, that in any teaching or learning situation basic perceptual capacities come into play. These capacities are usually simply assumed and this explains why, at least in part, they are so often overlooked. However, if our assumptions are mistaken and the student does *not* for some reason possess the perceptual concept, he must either be taught it or come to acquire it on his own. Otherwise, certain further learning will simply not be possible. There are, in all teaching and learning, perceptual capacities which are either presupposed or must themselves be taught or otherwise learned.

I believe my initial examples are illustrations of the failure of our normally smoothly working perceptual capacities. They are examples of the necessity for some teaching and learning of *perceptions.* Thus, the black teenagers do not see their conduct as unlawful or even annoying. They are playing around and do not intend to harm anyone. If they bump into someone occasionally, it is an accident. Unless they can come to see their behavior as possibly harmful to passersby, for them there will be no logical explanation for what the police are doing but harassment. The police, on the other hand—because of their training, their fears, and possibly their prejudices—see the law's being broken and the potentiality for a real blowup. Unless they can be brought to see the similarities between this case and, for example, the horsing around of a Shriner's convention, they will only reinforce their interpretation of blacks as disorderly.

The sophomore physics student may have an excellent grasp of physical theory, at least as it is exemplified by formulae and conceptual manipulation. However, until he sees the concepts at work in the problems at the end of the chapter, he has not fully mastered his lesson. There is, in principle, no way in which a mechanical recipe can be given him to apply the theory to the problems. Rather, his perceptual experience must come to him organized under the categories of the theory he has learned. Again, the learning of new perceptions is required.

The prospective teacher needs to develop philosophical perspectives about teaching. He needs new perspectives, for example, which will enable him to see contract negotiations in the light of the professor's analysis of teaching. For if one is arguing over what duties can be taken over by teacher's aides or other paraprofessionals, the ability to see which actions fall under the concept of teaching and which do not is crucial. Is writing an assignment on the chalkboard "teaching"? Or must the teacher be engaged in a dialogue with the students to be "teaching"? The student needs to learn some new perceptions here. Concomitantly, the professor needs to realize that what is obvious to him because he is already operating with a certain set of perceptual categories may be completely foreign to the students because they cannot yet organize their perceptual experience in the appropriate ways.

The recipe-follower does not have the perceptual category of the proper "feel" of the dough. It is not that one must learn cognitively all the varying circumstances (they are probably indefinite in number anyway) which can alter the proportions of flour and liquid in a recipe. What is needed is to fix the perceptual category of the proper feel so that more flour (or more liquid) can be added as needed, *regardless* of the underlying reason why it is needed. A new perception, not more inferences, must be learned.

The duck-rabbit case is a paradigm example of the necessity for acquiring a new perception. The rabbit-aspect blind person quite clearly does not need to infer that the rabbit is looking up. He sees that when he sees the rabbit, and the switching back and forth of the perceptual gestalt when one sees first the duck, then the rabbit, and so on, is a clear case of differing perceptions.

Finally, it would be absurd to suppose that the young teacher in the newly integrated classroom merely needs to draw the correct inferences about the relative activity of blacks and whites in his classroom. He simply cannot see the whites acting up; or, conversely, he cannot see youthful exuberance in the black children's behavior. He too needs a new set of *perceptions.*

It will help to note at this point that these fairly ordinary examples of mine are instances of some quite well-known and long-standing educational issues. Perhaps most obvious is the problem of relevance. My example of the prospective teacher and the philosophy of education professor is a clear-cut instance of a case in which one could argue over whether or not the material being taught and learned is relevant.

Another familiar problem area exemplified by my series is that of understanding different cultures—a problem epitomized by the oft-heard claim that a nonmember of the culture cannot really understand it. Both the street incident and the teacher in the desegregated classroom are examples here. At a minimum, the claim is made that abstract learning in such cases must be supplemented by "real" experience. Indeed, the problem is probably not limited to that of understanding different cultures, but appears also in the more general guise of various efforts to "learn by doing." So the whole area of field trips and practical experience is relevant here too.

Another example of a problem area is the constantly recurring difficulty of translating theory into practice. As a case like that of the physics student seems to indicate, it is not so that the theory isn't "really" understood until the student can do the problems. It is rather that perceptual experience must come to be organized in accordance with the theory before it can be applied. All of the so-called clinical disciplines face this problem. A good deal of practice seems to be required to enable the student to perceive the field through the cognitive lenses provided by the discipline. My guess is that when successful, student teaching makes use of precisely such a training in perceptual organization or reorganization of the student teacher's experience.

In its pure form this problem resolves itself into the problem of abstraction and classification. If we are ever to move beyond the mere *having* of experience—even to the level of saying that *this* experience today is the same kind of experience as *that* experience yesterday— then we are forced to classify. We abstract from the existential fullness of the experience and say that it is in virtue of this or that feature, which is the same in the two cases, that the experiences are experiences of the same kind. Thus there arises a very primitive kind of classification. It is in this sense that classification is often listed as a very basic kind of theorizing.² The emphasis here is usually on the difficulties involved in coming up with fruitful classifications; but even so the implication is still present that there must *be* something to be classified—and occasionally one's attention could be turned to that perceptual portion of the phenomenon rather than to the classifications themselves.

Need for Perceptual Learning

It may seem that I am covering familiar ground; and, in a certain sense, much of what I have said and will say will sound superficially like what has been said many times before. It is therefore absolutely crucial to understand the difference in the way in which I am treating these topics. My contention is that each and every one of these problems, specific or general, requires *perceptual* learning. The traditional treatment of these areas usually takes perception as unproblematic and locates the difficulties in the interpretations given to the perceptions. Even when the problem clearly involves perceptions, the general belief is that one need only arrange the conditions of the experience and the perceptions will take care of themselves. A moment's reflection on my examples will show that, with the possible exception of the duck-rabbit case, the standard view of these situations is that perception is not the problem. Rather it is considered to be the interpretations put on and inferences drawn from the perception.

On the standard view it is argued that surely at some level both the black teenagers and the policemen see the same street scene and because of different biases interpret it differently. The physics student sees the problem but doesn't know how to apply the theory. The prospective teacher can see acts of teaching; he just can't understand the purpose of conceptualizing it as his professor wishes him to. The professor *has* applied those concepts to the same teaching both he and the student perceive. Even the "feel" of the dough to the experienced cook is the result of an inference from other basic perceptions of "elasticity" in other contexts. In the case of the duck-rabbit, all we really see is lines and we infer first to the duck and then to the rabbit.

---

² See, for example, Richard Rudner, *Philosophy of Social Science* (Englewood Cliffs, N.J.: Prentice-Hall, 1966), Chapter 2.

The new teacher sees the activity of both whites and blacks, but because of his prejudices and fears interprets the activity of the blacks in a different way.

Familiar as this standard view is, I repeat that I believe it to be almost wholly mistaken. Before I turn to the defense of my claim that these examples are examples of *perceptual* problems rather than *interpretive* problems, let me try to indicate the difference I am getting at when I use the terms "perception" and "interpretation." Consider the following contrasts:

Fact	Theory
Observation	Interpretation
Data	Inference
Perception	Cognition
Input	Program
Sensation	Perception

In each case the teaching or learning of something in the right-hand column depends on or presupposes the capacity to acquire by means of the senses the things in the left-hand column. One cannot teach a theory without presupposing that the student knows what kind of facts the theory is supposed to account for. An interpretation is always an interpretation *of* something already (perceptually) in hand. We make inferences *from* our data; cognition depends on perception. Inputs are processed by programs and sensations are integrated in perceptions. To paraphrase Kant, cognition would be empty without perception.[3]

Because of the wide variation in terminology, I am not overly concerned about giving here a very precise characterization of a theory or a fact.[4] I am rather concerned with the distinction between *what* we perceive and the inferences we draw on the basis of what we perceive—the distinction between *seeing* and *interpreting* what is seen. Being completely clear on this distinction is extremely difficult and is made more so by the fact that the term "perception" itself is

---

[3] Immanuel Kant, *Critique of Pure Reason,* tr. Norman Kemp Smith (London: Macmillan, 1961).
[4] See Chapter 1 for a fuller discussion of what is meant by "fact," "theory," and related terms in the literature.

sometimes used in the right-hand column to refer to the cognitive set taken up as a result of basic sensation.[5] For my purposes it will be sufficient if one simply thinks of the contrast between what is more or less given to us as a result of the standard operation of our senses on the one hand and the cognitive or conceptual or theoretical interpretations we give to this material on the other hand. What I am thus contending is that at least on occasion, teaching-learning problems center around what is *perceived* rather than on the *interpretations* or *theoretical explanations* we give of what is perceived.

Perception and Teaching

I now turn to the positive defense of my claim that what is essentially involved in these teaching-learning examples are perceptual problems. In support of this claim I will argue for the following three propositions:

1. In many cases it is simply not possible to give an account of the phenomenon in the standard way (i.e., in terms of a concept's being applied to a given unproblematic perception). Sometimes what is involved is the learning of a new perceptual category.
2. These new perceptual categories are not always merely different. Sometimes they are hierarchically arranged.
3. In a hierarchy of perceptions there is no ground-floor level of perceptions. *All* perception is conceptually loaded.

Let me try to make these points through a consideration of some of my introductory examples.

Perception and Conception

Recall the case of the would-be teacher who finds philosophy of education "irrelevant." (The case is easily generalized to other areas.) On the professor's side there is the danger of not recognizing the necessity of hooking up his theoretical expostulations with perceptual categories which the student actually possesses.[6] On the student's side

---

[5] Chapter 6 of this volume seems to use "perception" in this sense.
[6] See, for example, my "Learning with Understanding," in *Readings in the*

there is the danger that he will consider nothing relevant unless it gives him a recipe for dealing with his particular problems. And yet, as one can see even in the cooking example, recipes "work" only if one perceives the appropriate situations in which to use them. Slavishly following a recipe for a favorite bread utilizing a new kind of flour is sure to lead to disaster unless one has developed the perceptual category of the proper "feel" of the dough. It is only if one can modify the recipe to properly adjust proportions of liquid and flour that one can truly be said to know how to bake bread. Similarly, until the student develops perceptual categories for dealing with his practical experiences which go beyond mere recipes, he will not become a real teacher. In terms which Professor Mathis uses in this volume (Chapter 2), he may train his students, but he will be unable to teach them.

Prima facie, the concept of training is not synonymous with the concept of teaching, as the analogy with blindly following a recipe and being a good cook shows. *The situation is perceived differently in the two cases.* The cook may or may not add so many cups of water to so many cups of flour. It will depend on the consistency of the dough. The recipe-follower will add so many cups of flour regardless of the consistency. It is possible of course that if informed of the hardness of the flour, the recipe-follower may be able to infer that he should add more liquid. The point, however, is that the conclusion thus reached by inference is reached perceptually by the cook. The teacher may or may not give a mini-lecture on a certain topic depending on the flow of the discussion. The trainer will likely give the lecture regardless because that is what his "recipe" tells him. Again, he may be able to infer that he should give the lecture (if he has time), but the master teacher can *see* that he should. There are simply two different levels of observational categories working here.[7]

Two problems arise at this point. In the first place it might be

---

Philosophy of Education: A Study of Curriculum, ed. Jane R. Martin (Boston: Allyn and Bacon, 1970).

[7] See my "Theories Are Tested by Observing the Facts: Or Are They?" *Philosophical Redirection of Educational Research,* National Society for the Study of Education, 71st Yearbook, Part I (Chicago: University of Chicago, 1972), pp. 58–62, for a more detailed discussion of this and the following points.

objected that a behavioristic social science methodology constitutes an argument against what I have been saying. Human action, it would be argued, must be explained by referring it to observable behavior; and the "appropriateness" of a situation for a mini-lecture is not an observable piece of behavior. Rather the teacher can only observe such things as students asking questions and must infer to the appropriateness of the mini-lecture. This objection misunderstands my point. My argument for thinking there are different *perceptual* categories at work does not prejudge the issue of behaviorism. It would be perfectly compatible with what I have said for it to turn out some day that the mechanisms of behavior described in the behaviorists' favored observation language are what we must use to theoretically explain what the cook and teacher do. What I have pointed out is that what these two do is, *prima facie,* different from what the recipe-follower and trainer do. This difference must be accounted for in any adequate theory. And, as I shall argue below, the issue of what *can* be observed is not decidable independently of the theory. Thus the behaviorist cannot rule out *a priori* the possibility that the appropriateness of situations for mini-lectures is observable. The arguments I have offered do, however, rule out the possibility that behavioral accounts are all that we *mean* by cooking and teaching. But no serious behaviorist today, not even Skinner, would make such a naive claim.

Another analogy may help to show the difference between an account which tries to *definitionally reduce* a phenomenon to a set of favored terms and an account which *explains* the phenomenon in the favored terms. The kinetic theory of heat surely does not have the same meaning as ordinary statements we make about heat and cold. When Plato (or I) say it will be warmer tomorrow we certainly do not *mean* that air molecules will be moving faster. Plato knew nothing of air molecules and I know almost as little; yet surely what we say is sensible. Nevertheless, it is quite true that movement of air molecules is all that is involved in heat phenomena. Furthermore, the movement of molecules is connected with heat as I understand it without the concepts' being synonymous. Similarly, behavioral notions might account for my notions of cooking and teaching without being synonymous with them. What my arguments have done is to point out that such an account must be given.

The Believing in Seeing

In the second place, granting that I leave open the possibility of a behaviorism which accounts for, but does not define, cooking and teaching, it could be urged that it is still highly objectionable for me to speak of different perceptual categories. Surely the categories of the recipe-follower and the trainer are simply proper perceptual parts of the inferential categories of the cook and the teacher. *What* we see are flour and water being mixed and we *infer* the cook's concept of appropriate feel. *What* we see are mini-lectures and we *infer* the teacher's concept of the proper direction of the discussion. There is perception and inference, not different perceptions. Surely such an account squares with common sense. The judgments appropriate to the cook and the teacher are not, at least not all of them, *perceptual* judgments.

It is extremely important to see that this standard conception of the interface I am describing, no matter how commonsensical it may sound, is quite simply wrong. This point can be made most graphically with the duck-rabbit example. The standard account would be that we see the lines and infer the rabbit (or the duck). But this account is quite preposterous. In the first place, it is very difficult to see just the lines. Try it. If you succeed, it is nothing like removing an inference. Which one did you remove, the duck inference or the rabbit inference? How is it that the "same" lines lead to different inferences? The inference, if there were one, would surely have to be instantaneous since it takes no time at all to switch back and forth. Why call it an inference at all then? Indeed this kind of case is almost a paradigm example of a gestalt switch, which has long been widely recognized as a perceptual, not an inferential, phenomenon. The cook's "feel" for the dough is also clearly a *perceptual,* not an inferential, category, although the novice may well have to infer that *this* is the proper feel from his knowledge of the time he has kneaded and the flour he has used. If one sees the mini-lecture, then one sees something different from if one sees the teacher providing some background information to the discussion—even though the *trainer* may have to infer that by giving the mini-lecture he will be giving background information.[8]

[8] I do not here have the space to provide a more detailed and convincing exposition of the claim that what is involved are different *perceptual* categories. It will be sufficient for my purposes if the reader understands what it is I am

Perceptual Hierarchies

I turn now to my second point, namely, that these perceptual categories are sometimes hierarchically related. Consider the duck-rabbit again. Now it is true that when one sees the duck, one is seeing something which is *simply* different from when one sees the rabbit. There is no hierarchical arrangement here. However, with quite a bit of practice it is possible for some to see the duck-rabbit *simply* as a collection of lines. In this case seeing the duck-rabbit as a collection of lines and seeing it as a rabbit is an example of the hierarchical relationship. And remember, I have already shown that the hierarchy *need* not be one of perception and interpretation (although it may be—remember the inferences of the novice cook and the trainer).

The hierarchical relationship is obvious. In some sense or other the lines are involved in the rabbit; following the recipe is involved in

---

claiming. Then the implications of this perspective, which I will develop more fully in the remainder of the chapter, can also serve as an argument for my position. It is my belief that using this model of a perceptual hierarchy makes a good many otherwise puzzling things fall into place. If a more detailed direct discussion of perception vs. inference is desired, one might consult any of the following:

L. Wittgenstein, *Philosophical Investigation,* tr. G. E. M. Anscombe, 3rd ed. (New York: Macmillan, 1968), Part II.

Hugh G. Petrie, "Science and Metaphysics: A Wittgensteinian Interpretation," in *Essays on Wittgenstein,* ed. E. D. Klemke (Urbana: University of Illinois Press, 1971), pp. 138–169.

William Powers, *Behavior: The Control of Perception* (Aldine, forthcoming).

N. R. Hanson, *Patterns of Discovery* (London: Cambridge University Press, 1958).

W. V. O. Quine, *Word and Object* (New York: John Wiley and Sons, 1960).

Stephen Toulmin, *Foresight and Understanding* (New York: Harper Torch Books, 1961).

T. S. Kuhn, *The Structure of Scientific Revolutions* (Chicago: University of Chicago Press, 1962).

Hugh G. Petrie, *The Logical Effects of Theory on Observational Categories,* Office of Education Contract 0-8-080023-3669(010).

K. Koffka, *Principles of Gestalt Psychology* (New York: Harcourt, Brace and World, 1935).

W. Kohler, *Gestalt Psychology* (New York: Liveright, 1947).

the cook's performance; and giving the mini-lecture is involved in the teacher's giving of background information. Yet this "involvement" is not one of "being a proper part of." That this is so is quite obvious in the case of the duck-rabbit, for there is nothing else *there* which could serve as the "rest" of the perception in the case of seeing the duck as over against the lines. Yet in a quite clear experiential sense we *perceive* something different when we see the lines and when we see the duck. I think the same thing holds true in the cooking and teaching cases. There is nothing more to the cook's activities than adding flour and liquid and kneading for a period of time, and yet what the cook can be observed to be doing is different from what the novice can be observed to be doing. There is nothing more to the teacher's giving background information than the mini-lecture and yet that is not what he is observably doing.

It is certainly true that the lines, the adding of flour and water, and the mini-lecture all must be present in order to see the duck, "feel" the dough, and give the background information; but these are not what is observable in the hierarchical case. The way one tells if what is being perceived is the rabbit or the lines is by seeing what other perceptual connections the person is willing to make. If these connections are "rabbit-appropriate" (e.g., saying, "There are his ears"; putting the picture with other pictures of rabbits; showing you his pet rabbit, etc.), then he perceives a rabbit. If they are "line-appropriate" (e.g., he draws other abstract systems of lines), then he sees the lines. If the connections are "cook-appropriate" (e.g., saying, "the flour must be harder"; adding more or less liquid; kneading a longer or shorter time; consistently coming out with good bread, etc.), then the person "feels" the dough. If the connections are "recipe-appropriate" (e.g., slavish following of the recipe; inconsistent results; inability to adapt to new circumstances, etc.), then following the recipe is perceived. If the connections are "teacher-appropriate" (e.g., not giving the lecture in another circumstance; varying responses to suit the circumstances; being able to explain why he gave the lecture in terms of some overall goal, etc.), then his perception was of giving background information. If the connections are "trainer-appropriate" (e.g., rote drill, etc.), then the perception is of the mini-lecture.

And, of course, we can make mistakes in attributing perceptions. We would be apprised of our mistakes precisely by the kinds of "appropriateness" criteria listed above. It also remains true that what one person simply perceives, another (usually with less experience and knowledge) needs to infer.

Ground-Floor Levels of Perception

I now turn to my final claim that in this hierarchy there is no ground floor of perceptions. Let me do so by means of considering one more objection. Even granting that there really is a hierarchy of perceptual categories and not just a hierarchy of perception and inference, still, perceptual categories are more or less determinate. Therefore, if what we need is to obtain some perceptual learning in some of the cases under discussion, then we either expose the student to the appropriate experiences, or, if that is too difficult, we can be more sophisticated with audiovisual aids or even our descriptions of what the perceptions would be like. After all, field trips have been around for quite a while.

The response here is that the evidence shows that perceptual categories, at least in many interesting cases—and I think in all of my examples—are *not* more or less determinate. Consider the duck-rabbit again. One can show the student this picture time and again and even say "rabbit, rabbit" over and over and still fail to have the desired perceptual learning take place. The student's ability to see a rabbit depends on his ability to organize the lines into a rabbit perception and, until he can form that gestalt, the perception will *not* be determinate in the required way. Until he knows what rabbits are and can use that knowledge to organize his perceptual field, he cannot see the picture as a rabbit. It might be thought that the lines are in some sense more basic than the rabbit as perceptual categories. This may be so, but they are not ultimately basic because one *could* be mistaken about them, too. (Consider some primitive who might see "lines" as magic of the gods.) As long as the possibility of mistake remains, the categories seem not to be "basic" perceptually. And as the sorry history of sense-data theories shows, mistakes always seem possible—at least if one wants to do anything more than point at fleeting experiences. One cannot even classify them without the possibility of mistake. In short, observational categories are theory-dependent and there is no basic predeterminable set of observational categories to which we can refer.[9]

I now have another way of identifying the problem common to my introductory examples. Given a theory-loaded hierarchy of perceptual categories with no basic set passively accessible merely through experience, it follows that the problem in the examples is that the appropriate perceptual categories together with the appropriate theory have not been learned or taught. Perceptual experience has not yet hooked up with theory because the theory has not yet structured the perceptual experience so that it *can* hook up. The concept of law and order when used by the police and when used by the ghetto resident involves their *seeing* different things. The college physics student needs to see his problems in terms of kinetic theory. The prospective teachers need to see in their activities the logical effects of teaching traced by their professor. The novice must come to feel the dough for consistency. The person knowing about rabbits must see the rabbit looking up. The young teacher really does need to become color blind and not merely say he is, so that the black faces in his classroom do not call his attention to excess activity.

Relating Theory to Perception

Let me try to drive home the point about the necessity for bringing theory to bear *in* perception before the learning can be considered to be complete, by means of extended consideration of a new example. David Nyberg describes a perfect case.[10] Nyberg was called upon to do some small group work with a group of educational planners. These

---

[9] See my "A Dogma of Operationalism in the Social Sciences," *Philosophy of the Social Sciences,* Vol. 1 (1971), pp. 145–160 for a detailed discussion of the impossibility of finding a basic set of observational categories. If one is worried about the incipient radical subjectivism in this view, see my "Science and Metaphysics: A Wittgensteinian Interpretation," note 8, for a way of saving objectivity.

[10] David Nyberg, *Tough and Tender Learning* (Palo Alto, Calif.: National Press Books, 1971), Chapter 7.

people worked mostly in urban school districts, and a major common concern was how they as professionals could convince the community, mainly poor and disadvantaged, that the school was doing the right things for the community. Nyberg set up two rules for his group experience:

> (1) If we could not talk about something that was happening at the present time, inside this room, then we would remain silent; no talk about the past, the future, or about persons outside the room would be allowed. (2) Whenever we spoke we would address ourselves to one other person and look him in the eyes while we were speaking; talking to the group in general (as I was doing then) or talking to oneself would not be allowed.[11]

What followed was sheer hell—long periods of silence, anger, feelings of a waste of time, total inability to follow the rules, hostility toward the leader, Nyberg, and so on. After a long period Nyberg called off the exercise and made his points. He, Nyberg, had set the rules and forced the participants to talk, if they wanted to talk at all, in an unfamiliar language—a "whole person" language in which thought and feeling and action merge. He did not allow them to use their more comfortable "head" language—their professional-theoretical language. He had in effect put them in the position that they had so often put their communities into during meetings. Nyberg had made them mad by imposing the rules just as they had so often, so unwittingly, made their communities mad by imposing the rules. When this sank in, the participants began to see their former actions in a new light.

The points I wish to make about this story are just slightly different from Nyberg's. The first point concerns what occurred *within* the experience. The "head" language used by the educational planners does not generally structure the perceptions of the community. It is jargon in the worst sense and not understood. The community, although in some sense talking about the "same" things, their schools and children, are nevertheless perceiving different things from the

[11] *Ibid.*, pp. 87–88.

planners. And no amount of "mere" exposure or experience will guarantee or even make likely that the perceptual experiences of the two groups will coincide.

My second point is *about* Nyberg's experience. One could have talked to these planners till doomsday about different perceptions of the schools—talk which most likely would have been interpreted by them in terms of their "head" language so that they never would have been able to restructure their perceptual experience appropriately. What was needed was the learning of new perceptions. By a clever role reversal, Nyberg structured the situation so that the planners would almost surely have to experience the same kinds of things their respective communities experienced—anger, frustration, etc. Then if he could only connect that experience with the theoretical points he was making, his total teaching job would be a success, as, apparently, it was. He recognized that an important part of his teaching task involved the restructuring of perceptions and recognized further that if he remained solely in a head language, the planners' perceptions would also be in a head language and he would thus utterly fail. In *this* case Nyberg could not utilize the standard perceptions these planners would bring to bear. He had an important perceptual learning component with which to deal. He had to get the planners actually to "practice" feeling like members of the community cut off from using their own language by some supposed expert. Notice that this practice was not simply some kind of rote drill, but rather a very directed practice which took full account of the theoretical effects on perceptual categories.

It should be noted further that the learning of new perceptual categories, especially when it occurs in an accelerated way, as in the example, is a very emotional experience. Rather than open up and allow experience organized in the new way to just happen, people typically react in a very hostile and defensive way. And, of course, this is perfectly understandable. What you are asking them to do, in a very short space of time, is to structure their perceptual experience in new and partially unknown ways. Man has a natural fear of the unknown, and willingly to put himself into a situation where he may not know what's coming next is quite a bit to ask.

The problem is made doubly serious by the fact that if one does *not* force a situation in which the perceptual reorganization or experience is a likely response, then the likelihood that the students will simply continue assimilating the experience in their old categories is greatly increased. For if, as is usually the case, the teacher avoids any explicit attention to the perceptual component, hoping it will take care of itself, the perceptual learning usually does not take place and the experience is assimilated in the old perceptual categories. When this occurs it is especially difficult to recognize because usually the *conceptual* categories of the new learning *are* assimilated and used more or less correctly. These conceptual categories are what are usually involved in standard testing instruments to determine if learning has taken place. The distortions caused by utilizing the new conceptions with the old perceptions show up in practice long after the formal classroom teaching and learning. Might this be part of the explanation of how people can say of a straight-A student, "Don't they teach them anything at college these days?" It also explains why ordinary lecture presentations to educational leaders such as those in Nyberg's example usually have no lasting effect. Even if *told* that their constituents talk a different language, these people process that information in their old-fashioned perceptual terms and the truly far-reaching effects of the perceptual diversity cannot be fully appreciated by them. Quite literally, while looking at the "same" things as their constituents, they see different things.

Thus there is a serious strategic problem facing the teacher who correctly identifies a perceptual component as one of his goals. He must ask himself, "Can I develop the categories in slow, easy stages to minimize the emotional impact, or must I attempt to force a situation in which perceptual reorganization is probable, realizing I may lose the class (or my job) from the resulting emotional upheaval?"

More importantly, however one wishes to analyze value judgments and their relationship to factual judgments, it must be obvious that in the area of basic perceptual reorganization, one is facing a serious value problem. Even assuming perceptions are somehow ethically neutral, they quickly hook up with basic ethical principles—and different ones will hook up in different ways. Moreover, it is clearly a value decision in a broad sense as to which of a competing set of perceptual categories is "better." Thus the teacher can avoid making value judgments only through allowing the perceptual base of what he is trying to teach possibly to be distorted through the perceptual lenses of the student if these are inappropriate.

However, nothing I have said gives any guarantee that the teacher can bring the student to view the world through just any arbitrary set of categories. Indeed, because of the deep emotional involvement with one's basic way of viewing the world, nothing is harder than to change perceptions. Even if one abstracts from the merely emotional attachment or considers someone, such as a child, who does not yet have a way of viewing the world, the teacher still does not have *carte blanche*. Some ways of viewing the world just don't work and occasionally the student may know this better than the teacher. What I am trying to emphasize here is the extreme depth of the psychological and ethical problems the teacher is committed to if he seriously takes perceptual reorganization as one of his goals.

Perceptions, Goals, and Teaching Strategies

I now want to apply this view of the learning of perceptions to an influential current idea concerning the relationship between goals and teaching strategies. I refer to the view that teaching outcomes should be written in terms of behavioral objectives and that teaching strategies should be designed to bring about these fairly specific behavioral objectives. The standard view is that these objectives can be precisely specified and unambiguously observed when and if they occur. Learning theory and teaching theory can then supply the empirical laws connecting these goal behaviors with fairly specific teaching behaviors so that we can know which teaching behaviors to initiate to bring about the desired outcomes.

It must be obvious that with my rejection of any unique set of observation categories I also reject the notion of being able to specify some sort of determinate behavior which can properly count as an educational goal. To do so would be to revert to the recipe-following model of perceptual categories. However, the thrust of the behavioral-objectives people is not incompatible with the views developed in this chapter. It is a consequence of my position that one may very well be able to observe a teacher "making a point," rather than observe the teacher saying thus and so and inferring to his making a point. Thus, since all observational categories are theory-loaded, there is no reason not to specify *indices* of educational goals in observational categories which have something to do with education rather than in parrot-like categories. Let us not confuse the desirable characteristic of specifying goals clearly with a particular favored observation language. Let us specify our goals in the observational language of *education* rather than in the observational language of a particular (behavioral) social science. These languages may ultimately be related, but for now the hierarchical view of perceptual categories demands that we not mix our categories (and hence our theories). If we do, we simply succeed in talking past one another.[12]

Those who criticize behavioral objectives are surely right in wanting to know what in the world the typical behavioral specification has to do with education. They sense, however vaguely, that the observational categories of education are *not* the observational categories of current behavior theory. They go too far, however, in asserting that education can have no observable outcomes at all. They have been taken in at least partly by the behavioral-objectives people. They seem to feel that if education's observational categories are not behavioristic, then they must not be observational at all. In short, they cut off their theory from organizing perceptual experience in categories which would be appropriate.

Conversely, those who are currently pushing behavioral objectives seem to err in just the opposite way. They see the necessity for theory to hook up with observational categories so that it can be *about* something rather than just floating in air. But they tack onto this insight the philosophically and psychologically discredited belief that there is one favored *given* set of observational categories to be used—namely a behavioristic set.[13] With such a limited set of observational categories, the behavioral-objectives people tend to

---

[12] See my "Why Has Learning Theory Failed to Teach Us How to Learn," *Proceedings of the Philosophy of Education Society* (1969), pp. 163–170.

[13] Petrie, "A Dogma of Operationalism in the Social Sciences," *op. cit.* (above, note 9).

conflate the goal with the indices of the goal. One sees something quite different when one sees the giving of the mini-lecture *simpliciter* from when one sees it *as* providing background information. In the former case, if the lecture was not given the teacher has thus failed. In the latter case, the mere nonpresentation of the lecture does not imply the teacher has failed, although it can, in conjunction with collateral information, be used as one indication of failure. In conjunction with different collateral information, the failure to give the lecture would be an indication of success (e.g., if it could be shown the students already knew that part of the course, that the teacher recognized this, and thus knew he needn't give the mini-lecture). It would not be stretching things too much to liken insisting on giving educational objectives in strictly behavioral terms to insisting on identifying cooking with following recipes. The view of observational categories as hierarchical and theory-dependent with no "givenness" about them seems to do justice both to the insistence on observability of the pro-behavioral-objectives people and to the insistence on appropriateness of the anti-behavioral-objectives people.

Implications for the Teacher

What, then, should a teacher do? He should by all means be clear on the goals that he wishes to achieve; and this includes not only the cognitive goals he wishes his students to achieve, but also what perceptual categories these cognitive goals will imply his students must have. He will have to make psychological and ethical judgments on the costs involved in achieving his goals. He will also have to ask what sorts of evidence would indicate to him that both the cognitive goals *and* appropriate perceptual categories had been achieved by his students. He must be especially careful to determine if it is likely that the evidence he could get might turn out to be ambiguous. Might the "same" evidence be compatible both with really having achieved all the goals and with not having achieved them? The example of moral education is particularly appropriate here. If one has as a goal the attainment of certain moral principles where this includes the sensitivity to see when these moral principles apply, then success on a paper-and-pencil test concerning reasoning with the moral principles may not indicate that one has succeeded in educating a moral person. One will also have to see if the appropriate perceptions are present in the appropriate cases.

In other words, the teacher must ask what *perceptual* learning is required to reach his goal and what evidence is needed of *that*. Typically the evidence is not identical with the evidence which would indicate concomitant cognitive learning. To complicate matters even further, one also needs to ask whether the necessary perceptual learnings can be constructed out of the perceptual categories already reasonably attributable to the student or whether the categories the student already has are more likely to get in the way. Learning to do the problems at the end of the chapter in the physics book is probably an example of the former, while Nyberg's experiment is an example of the latter. Teaching strategies would need to be much different in the two cases.

In conclusion let me return now to my original examples to try to give some flavor of what all the foregoing means in particular cases. The ghetto street incident involves a radical clash of perceptions. There probably is no way one can build on the existing perceptions of either the police or the blacks to reach some common ground. Something radical like the form of the Nyberg case (or recently reported experiments of having the staff of mental hospitals actually *be* patients for a short time, or of law officers going to prison and actually experiencing the feelings of inmates) is what would be needed. Perhaps if the police could be put into the position of being hassled for something which is mildly irritating to others, but nevertheless a more or less acceptable part of their culture, the requisite perceptions could be gained. Perhaps a sergeant could crack down on police locker room horseplay. On the other hand, the black teenagers would need to be placed in a situation where someone else's "playing around" caused some minor inconvenience to them. This is the structure of the kind of experience which might work. There could be no guarantees—especially in a short-term experience—but at least the logic of what is needed is clear.

The sophomore physics student just needs practice. He can probably restructure his existing stock of perceptual categories with a little

The Believing in Seeing

more experience. In other words, the tradition of "homework," graded or not, but at least required, is probably educationally very sound. If one keeps clearly in mind the purpose of homework as providing practice in attaining appropriate perceptual categories, then traditional abuses such as using it for busy work or making it too routinized can perhaps be avoided.

The case of the required philosophy of education course presents a host of problems. It is certainly true that most academic disciplines have by now become *so* specialized and *so* arcane that they are capable of generating their own problems independently of any connection these problems might have with ordinary human experience. To this extent the students are surely correct in decrying the lack of relevance. The perceptual categories in use by many disciplines do not manage to engage perceptual categories lower down in the hierarchy in any way. It is as if one tried to deny that the mini-lecture had *anything* to do with providing background information instead of recognizing, as I have tried to do, that the two are not identical. This is doubtless the kernel of truth in the "romantic" criticisms of scholarly work being *too* objective and *too* cut off from the whole of life. The lower levels of the hierarchy of perceptual categories have been cut off.

On the other hand, as I have already indicated, the students are surely wrong in believing that the work of the professor is irrelevant to their concerns. What they need is some perceptual learning which would enable them to see their concerns in the categories of the scholarly discipline. If they would view their assignments more in the light of perceptual learning, rather than in terms of a waste of time, perhaps they could show more forbearance in condemning any course as irrelevant. It sometimes happens that the "relevance" appears only later—when experience begins coming in terms of the new perceptual categories which were learned. For his part the professor might take as a criterion of adequacy of his teaching and research that he can show an interested layman in some reasonable period of time what relevance his work has for common human problems.

The novice cook needs to practice making bread, preferably with a master cook who can point out when the dough has the right feel and then let the novice *feel* it. Of course, the novice could learn simply by doing if he can identify certain "feels" with certain outcomes and other "feels" with other outcomes. However, it is much harder, typically, to figure out one's own standard of reference than it is to have one provided. Perhaps a mixture of both doing it yourself and having some guidance is appropriate for school situations, which fall short of the creative work done on the frontiers of knowledge.

The person who is rabbit-aspect blind needs to have some contextual training. He needs to spatially orient the picture and to see it in contexts with rabbits, other pictures of rabbits (perhaps more realistic ones), to encounter the picture in conjunction with descriptions of rabbits and so on. This case illustrates a fairly basic level of coming to possess perceptual categories and is probably the closest of all to a straightforward stimulus-response paradigm. The important thing to note here is that even in so simple a case it is not logically possible to eliminate all traces of ambiguity and misperception. It may be the case that we ought to make finer perceptual distinctions in rabbits (perhaps sexual ones) than we do. On the other hand, perhaps we would do better to see rabbits as rodents in general, or maybe even as the useless stuff attached to rabbit feet. While the foregoing examples are surely fanciful, many others are not. In social science methodology, do we perceive a certain treatment given to an experimental group as a pretest or as practice? Until we can see it as possibly the latter, the justification of the simplest kind of control groups will be incomprehensible to us.

The white teacher with the black "hyperactive" children needs a good in-service program to help him with his racial perceptions. Perhaps one might design an experience where all the children in his class wore effective disguises for a day so he couldn't tell their race. (Voice, mannerisms, and so on would also have to be disguised.) Then see if he could pick out the hyperactive students by race. He could probably also use some seminars on black culture and modes of expression. Perhaps a film of his own activities along with some role playing would also help.

Indeed role playing, sensitivity training, and other such "affective" modes of teaching are put into a new light by the analysis of this paper. The insight they embody is not just that the affective as well as the cognitive is important and nice; but rather, since experience and cognition interact, experiences such as these are necessary to flesh out cognitive theories with perceptual categories. Such experiences are thus best viewed not as ends in themselves but rather as sometimes effective means of perceptual learning in which perceptual learning gives substance to our cognitive learning and vice versa.

When we realize that our perceptual categories form a "bottomless" hierarchy which is at all points theory-laden, which cannot be passively acquired, and which sometimes leads us astray in our attempts to communicate, then we will have a chance of recognizing the importance of perceptual learning and the teaching of perceptual categories and judgments in conjunction with our educational goals. The point is this: without explicit attention to the perceptual aspects of teaching and learning situations, our instructional efforts will be processed in terms of whatever categories the student happens to have, whether these are appropriate or not. If, on the other hand, we realize the effects perceptions and judgments have on each other, we have a chance of designing our instructional efforts so that the role of perception will not be ignored. We can and sometimes must educate our basic perceptions and not just the inferences we draw on the basis of perception.

4 Systems Conflict in the Learning Alliance

PAUL BOHANNAN, WILLIAM POWERS, and MARK SCHOEPFLE

There are several professions whose practitioners use the self—the entire personality—as their working tool: psychotherapy, ethnographic field research, and teaching. Both psychotherapy and ethnography have been vastly improved by the fact that the activities of the practitioners have been thoroughly checked out for control of conflict. Conflict in the teacher's realm is far less well understood.

Some of the ideas developed in one of these professions for checking out the tool-kit, as it were, for doing the job—specifically, for avoiding conflict—can be transferred (at least by analogy) to the others. Thus our purpose here is to investigate some of the principles worked out by psychotherapists and ethnographers for understanding conflict and dealing with themselves in situations of conflict. How do these professionals use themselves and even their very problems to help them do their jobs rather than as partisans in a conflict? We shall also make some suggestions about some of the ways in which this kind of information can be transformed or altered by teachers so that it fits their profession and their problems.

We shall first concentrate on two points: (1) the therapeutic alliance, as that relationship is practiced by psychoanalysts, and the way psychoanalysts deal with the problem of countertransference; (2) the ethnographic alliance, as that relationship is practiced by ethnographers, and the way ethnographers deal with the problem of culture shock. Both countertransference and culture shock are the best tools their practitioners can use, if they know how to do it. We shall then proceed to (3) the learning alliance and ways teachers can profit from the problem of conflict.

The Therapeutic Alliance

Psychoanalysts and other therapists have long recognized that therapy cannot take place if an alliance does not exist between the therapist and the patient to bring it about. Such an alliance calls for a certain type of commitment on the part of both parties to it : it calls for great skill and sensitivity on the part of the therapist—and calls for far lesser skills but no less commitment on the part of the patient.

Fundamentally, the patient must be willing to enter into an alliance with the therapist to work toward the goal of his own enlightenment and ultimate greater satisfaction and pleasure in his own behavior. Unless the patient can make such a commitment, most therapists will not accept him as a patient. There are comparatively few things a therapist can do to develop in a patient the capacity or willingness to enter into a therapeutic alliance. But there are many, many things she [1] can do to destroy that capacity and willingness.

The alliance, as a dyad, must show a number of characteristics :

1. A readiness on the part of both patient and therapist to deal with a positive transference.
2. The patient's wish to recover.
3. The therapist's professional curiosity; her willingness to invest her time, energy, and regard in this person; and her capacity to deal with countertransference.

The therapist has several advantages over the teacher. She can dismiss a patient who cannot play his part in an alliance—and she can do so without allowing herself the luxury of guilt. Some people cannot be helped by therapy—or at least by this particular therapist. If the therapist recognizes that, she does everyone a favor by dismissing the patient. If she does not recognize it when it is in fact the case, she is incompetent.

---

[1] Throughout, the pronoun "she" refers to therapist, ethnographer, or teacher. The pronoun "he" refers to patient, informant, or student.

Initial Intervention

One of the most important events in a psychotherapy is the therapist's first intervention. It sets the tone for many sessions to come. If that first intervention is premature, it may very well interfere with the therapeutic transference. The patient may not be ready to receive the message that the therapist gives him—but past the point at which he can merely blot it out. He is thereupon thrust back on his defenses. These defenses are enlightening to the therapist. After all, assisting the patient in removing defenses is ultimately the therapist's job; for most neuroses are defenses, rather than what lies behind the defenses. But one of the defenses may be to withdraw from participation in the alliance. Usually no single misinterpretation—not even the first one—is capable of holding up therapy for very long; but the therapist must be very careful to nurture the alliance at first. Eventually it will be strong enough to take all kinds of knocks, as trust is developed, as the strands of the relationship become manifold.

Blind Spots

The next point is that the therapist must never cooperate unconsciously with the patient's problem.

There is a blind spot at the point at which the optic nerve enters the eyeball. At that point, there are no receptor cones—obviously, because something else is there. Although we are never aware of our blind spots, because we have two eyes and stereoscopic vision, there are simple experiments by which people can be made aware of them. A psychic blind spot is an analogy—it is a point about which a person is "blind" presumably (to extend the metaphor) because it is too close to the nerve.

The only indication that any good therapist has that something is going on in one of her blind spots is that the therapy is not going well and she does not know why. At this point, she may try first one and then another explanation. None helps. Any good therapist in such a situation owes it to herself and to her patient to go to a third party—a colleague of the therapist who, in this role, is called her "supervisor"—to discuss the matter. A good supervisor can usually pick out the blind spot quickly and show the therapist what is happening. Most therapists need supervision from time to time throughout their careers. In another image, it is something like the vocal coach. A singer cannot hear her own voice as it is heard by others. Every singer must depend upon a vocal coach to tell her when she is achieving the result she wants—as well as when things are going wrong and not coming out quite as she intended.

Countertransference

The therapist must develop a sure, firm knowledge that she and the patient are in a social relationship. Following upon that, the therapist must know that the patient will, as he is gently frustrated in this relationship, transfer on to her the ideas and modes of behavior that were originally formed or were appropriate in other relationships. This is called the "transference." The therapist cannot, however, undergo the experience of being a "transference object" without having her own reactions to it. One of the therapist's tasks is to keep her own reactions constantly under her own scanning eye in order to understand those reactions in herself. Only in this way can she be sure that she does not cooperate with the patient's problems.

The therapist's reaction is called a countertransference. It differs from the transference in only one regard: the therapist has been carefully trained to observe the countertransference specifically so it does not interfere with an accurate observation and analysis of the transference.

In this way, the therapist is trained to turn her worst enemy (the countertransference) into her most reliable tool.

The Therapist and the Teacher

There are undoubtedly teachers who, at this stage in reading this article, want to say that they are teachers, not therapists, and that teachers should not get involved in therapy. We agree. Teachers should not get involved in psychotherapy—as teachers, they have to watch different points, do different things, which make it impossible even if they wanted to be therapists.

However, psychotherapists have developed certain techniques for using the self that can be usefully adapted to the classroom situation. The first of these techniques involves the sure, firm knowledge that teacher and student are in a social relationship—indeed, she is in a social relationship with each pupil, for all that sometimes they act as a group, and sometimes some of them join her vis-à-vis other students. (A social relationship is a situation in which two behaving organisms each alters its behavior because of the presence of the other.) In this relationship, the only key the teacher has to what is going on inside the pupil is to be found in knowing overtly and clearly what is happening to herself, and allowing herself to sense openly and clearly what her reactions are to the student's reactions to her behavior.

That being the case, she can create only half of the learning alliance—but it is far and away the bigger half, because it is the half in which things can most readily go wrong. However, she must admit that the student may be unteachable. A student is unteachable if he is not willing to enter into a learning alliance. Fundamentally, the pupil must be able to enter into an alliance with the teacher to work toward the goal of his own enlightenment and his greater pleasure in his own achievement.

There are two kinds of students marking the extremes of the range of attitudes: those in whom the willingness to enter a learning alliance is evident and those in whom it is not. Probably the eagerness to learn is never destroyed; but unwillingness to learn some things from some people in some circumstances can quite easily preclude a learning alliance with a particular teacher (or system) at a particular time. Thus, we think a totally unteachable pupil is rare—but there are many things that a teacher can do to destroy the pupil's capacity and willingness to learn. Our point is not to tell anyone how to make students want to learn, but to give guidance to teachers so that they will not destroy that willingness when it is present.

Before we go any further, we should make two points: (1) a student cannot be constrained to learn; and (2) a teacher must admit, when she decides that a student is unwilling to make an alliance, that it constitutes a failure of which she is a part (although perhaps not the root cause or even the efficient cause). There may be some students who will not learn in any school system—our only point is that before a teacher gives a student up, she should check herself and her school system out very thoroughly.

Learning and teaching are part of a single process. It is true that animals learn to do some things, like walking, without assistance or instruction—for instance, you cannot teach a child to walk, and yet it is difficult to teach him not to walk. You can, to a degree, teach him *how* to walk—how to hold and move his body. It is equally true that there are some things, such as reading a book, that a person can learn without a face-to-face social relationship. Nevertheless, in much of our learning process the demonstrator is vital. And learning from a demonstrator can be divided into two kinds of activities: what Gregory Bateson called proto-learning and deutero-learning.[2] Proto-learning, in teachers' terms, is learning a subject; deutero-learning is learning the context of proto-learning. To say that deutero-learning is "learning to learn" is correct, but over-simple. It includes cues for learning from the learning environment: learning to learn in some ways, in some situations, but not in others.

At this point in the discussion, it is important to recognize that the teacher can control only one person in the learning alliance—herself. She can control only a limited part of the learning environment (the building, the principal, and the school board are real). No teacher can *ever constrain* a change in the behavior of the student. Constraint, in a traditional sense, results when the first party reduces the field of interaction so that the choices open to the second party are narrowed. The ultimate choice is, of course, whether the other person decides to abide by the choices; tries to alter the choices; or breaks the relationship.

The relationship is difficult to break when the law says that the child must be bodily in the school building. The student is thereby reduced to a simpler choice: he can either buckle down and live with whatever choices he *can* make; or he can try, by whatever means at his disposal, to alter the field of choices. The teacher, of course, is doing the same thing. As we have just pointed out, no teacher can control the total learning environment—only her reaction to it and her behavior within it. Obviously, the student must enter into an alliance before his behavior can be altered. It is altered *only* because

[2] Gregory Bateson, "Social Planning and the Concept of Deutero-Learning," *Science, Philosophy and Religion, Second Symposium* (New York: Harper and Row, 1942); reprinted in Gregory Bateson, *Steps to an Ecology of Mind* (New York: Ballantine Books, 1972), pp. 159–176.

he chooses to alter it. The teacher usually cannot dismiss a student who cannot, or who refuses to, participate in the learning alliance—and hence when she fails, there is likely to be some guilt. This is a matter of the way in which each, therapist and teacher, learns to define her own job.

The curiosity of the therapist, her skill, regard, and thought—including unconscious thought—are at the command of fewer patients than most teachers have students, but each relationship is more intense. When a teacher has too many pupils, she does not have enough skill, regard, and thought—including unconscious thought—to put at the service of her profession. Dividing the supply up, measuring simply on a time basis, does not allow enough for each.

There should be, in our schools, someone who fulfills for teachers the function of the voice coach for singers or the supervisor for therapists. Obviously, the word "supervisor" is a dirty word in most school contexts, and the word "coach" means something very different. "Counselor" probably would not do, because counselors are traditionally for students instead of teachers. When we make up this new role, we must provide a name for it.

The Ethnographic Alliance

Anthropology is another profession in which the practitioner utilizes her entire personality in doing her job—at least this is the case in that portion of anthropology concerned with gathering ethnographic data. When an anthropologist goes into the field, she ideally investigates a culture that is strange to her, or a portion of a culture that she does not know well. In order to learn about this culture, she enters into close personal relationships with some people who know and practice the culture. She learns from them the way people do things.

The ethnographer employs a method that she calls participant observation. It is perhaps self-evident, yet important, to say that the essence of participant observation is twofold: the field worker must participate and she must observe. To participate she must take on one or more roles that a significant proportion of the community can accept. These roles are seldom defined by the community unless it is a fairly sophisticated community. Many communities today can accept without difficulty social scientists who take on the role of teacher or agency worker; many indeed can accept a person who appears in the role of an investigating social scientist. But, in other communities, a role must be built in the community itself. That takes time, because roles, to exist, must fit into role structures. Ideally, the participant's role is the least possibly disturbing to the other roles in the society. Yet, among those members of the community who eventually become the best informants, there is an unavoidable role change.

The informant's role, if it is to be more than casual, is taken on by people who are temperamentally able to raise the level of abstraction of their views and knowledge of their own culture. In order to be good informants, they have to think about their culture in a more abstract set of concepts than they need merely to live it. Some of these concepts may come from the anthropologist; some may come from the informant to explain his culture to himself; but many of them come from interaction.

The ethnographer must, obviously, have certain psychic as well as intellectual capacities in order to do the job. And she must learn not only the overt knowledge of the culture she is studying. She must also learn what Polanyi [3] called the "tacit knowledge," a dynamic sort of knowledge-by-doing that allows her to identify and act on something she perceives without ever taking time out to name it verbally.

Obviously, then, the ethnographer must be somebody who can learn on the spot—in what is to her a strange situation—with her entire sensing and learning apparatus. Her job is to learn and report what "they" do and what "they" say—their way of life, as entire as she can manage it. Learning in an ethnographic situation is not like learning to be a scientist, where there is a body of knowledge to be mastered. She must learn, rather, whatever it is that these people want to teach her. What they *want* to teach her is the most significant part of her data.

Obviously, then, when an anthropologist goes into a new culture

---

[3] Michael Polanyi, *The Tacit Dimension* (New York: Doubleday, 1966).

to make a study of it, she enters into close personal relationships with some people who know and practice that culture. She takes a cultured interest in the matters that the informant thinks are culturally interesting. Few informants can resist the temptation to "set her right" about the matter. Therefore, an anthropologist asks less of informants than therapists do of patients and far less than teachers do of students. She asks only to be accepted for herself (certainly she can never be accepted, for long at any rate, as anything else). And she then has the task of learning herself (as the instrument of learning), as she learns the way of life she came to study.

The point in this section is that in such a relationship the informant must "come up a level" of abstraction and learn to be comfortable with new insights into his own culture. The ethnographer, on the other hand, has to learn to deal with herself and her own values in an increasingly strange situation.

The Problem of Culture Shock

Ethnographers are as uncomfortable in unfamiliar cultural situations as anyone else. That cultural discomfort is part of the learning process. The danger is, of course, that the discomfort will become so great that the ethnographer will pull out—either physically leave the place, or spiritually close her receptivity. Once she does that, obviously, she can learn no more.

The task in training ethnographers, then, is to get them to realize when culture shock is affecting them: this is possible only for people who are in good touch with their own emotions, and who will admit that they have such emotions, even when it is "dishonorable" in terms of their own culture to admit them.

Thus, in this situation, it is the ethnographer, not the informant, who usually sets the boundaries of the relationship—since it is far more psychically demanding to live with strange and unpredictable values than it is to make your ideas and values more abstract by the statement of them. It may be a traumatic experience if the ethnographer must admit that she is no longer in control of even a portion of her environment. Everything she has taken for granted before—every implicit assumption about herself in relation to those around her—is brought into conflict and question. The possible symptoms of the culture shock that follows all too quickly are withdrawal, anger, homesickness, depression.

Ethnographers have to be spiritually prepared to know that these symptoms are what they work with. They are signals that there are gross discrepancies between their reference levels and what it is that they are actually experiencing. The ethnographic exercise means that the ethnographer must learn what reference level would be suitable for such experience. It certainly is not necessary that she adjust her own *personal* reference level—she adjusts *that* by the process of knowing how her personal reference levels would have to be altered if she were to live in this cultural system as a full participant. She therefore has two discrepancies: one between what she perceives and what she understands about *their* behavior; the second between the perceived error in the first discrepancy and what her standards are for her own behavior. Then, out of these discrepancies, which it is a higher order goal for her to understand, she must make the substance of her ethnographic report.

The Ethnographer and the Teacher

Culture shock occurs in situations other than during long stays in exotic lands. The depression and resentment that the recent (and not so recent) draftee feels in our military is an example from our own society. And let us remember that the young pupil in the classroom has been conscripted from kin and peer groups to interact in this strange social setting.

Thus the teacher and pupil are both trapped in a strange situation, and the pupil suffers immediate culture shock. The teacher may soon follow, especially if the students are from ethnic groups that are strange to her (even when she thinks she "knows" that group). Like the ethnographer, the teacher is trapped in the situation. To retreat would spell professional disaster. She gets angry, homesick, depressed—"How did I get into this?" she asks.

The malaise on both sides—student and teacher—is part of a learning process. The task of the teacher, like that of an ethnographer, is to realize when culture shock is affecting one's self. This is possible only for people who are in good touch with their own emotions, who can ask "Why am I bored? Why am I angry? Why am I anxious?" If the anthropologist or the teacher can begin the process of asking these questions, the answers she comes up with can tell her something about the people she is studying or teaching—and, at the same time something about herself. She will have utilized her emotions rather than merely suffering or abreacting them.

In a state of culture shock, the teacher has two choices (other than mere cowardly retreat): (1) she may seek the solace of her peers and explain her problems with the available pooled knowledge of her subculture; or (2) she may seek the help of an impartial outsider, a sort of ombudsman. The point of either action is to bring one's whole cultural knowledge into verbal awareness—in other words, to turn one's self into an informant about one's very own culture and personality.

The first of these choices is seldom satisfactory. The teacher-culture of any school is (not to put too fine an edge on it) a better or worse institutionalized defense mechanism. It lets teachers off the hook too easily. It gives them a ready-made explanation of their feelings before they have had an opportunity to check them out—and it usually does so at the expense of the reputation of the students. The teachers' lounge may be full of coffee and consolation, but it is also full of misinformation.

The other way, choosing to seek the help of the ombudsman, means that the teacher must (on her own hook in today's world) find somebody who is not an interested party to tell her what went wrong—not necessarily to tell her what she did wrong, but to help her analyze her own homesickness, anger, and depression. The ethnographer must do this with the very people she is studying if she is to generate the information that makes anthropology. The teacher does not have so easy an out. She can indeed use her pupils as informants from time to time, but she interacts with pupils in only a limited situation, on a "professional" basis. They cannot—and usually should not—become her confidants. The ethnographer using an ombudsman would be a failure—she would be giving to the ombudsman the raw material of her anthropology. The teacher, on the other hand, does not have the ethnographer option—she cannot make anthropology out of her raw material. Yet, despite these differences, there is much to be learned from the ethnographer about recognizing culture shock and something about how to handle the problems that arise from it.

The Learning Alliance

The learning alliance, like all alliances, is entered into because each party sees it as a means to satisfy his own goals. The durability of the alliance, therefore, depends on several factors: first, determining how it can be shaped so that it actually does satisfy these goals—and does so without creating more conflict than it resolves. Second, there must be sufficient communication between the parties to the alliance so that each can actually learn what the goals of the other are, and consequently adjust his own. It is not enough merely to brand the goals of students as inadequate or jejune or wrongheaded; an understanding of the countertransference tells us how to deal with that. It is not enough to be disgusted and self-righteous; an understanding of culture shock tells us that.

The difficulties in the learning alliance are subtle—they come, in large part, from considering only long-term goals without adequate attention to the short-term means for achieving them. The learning alliance is composed of short-term bargains as well as the overall long-term goals.

We are going to name this difficulty "systems conflict" because conflict is the first sign of the difficulty and because the conflict can occur, as it were invisibly, when the goal system of one party gets out of phase with the goal system of the other. This happens when, in focusing on the major alliance, the subordinate goals are not adequately bargained. Thus the separate bargains are vital to the alliance as a whole, because it is on the basis of bad bargains that systems conflict appears—and the whole alliance breaks down. The problem then becomes one of identifying the systems conflict and turning it into an ally.

The learning alliance concerns long-term and global agreement on goals such as "getting (or giving) an education" or "maintaining a friendly atmosphere." The difficulty arises, of course, because the short-term bargains may—if one is careless—work directly away from the main goals of the alliance. Perhaps "careless" is not the word: it implies accident and inattention. Most serious violations of the long-term alliance arise from what one does quite consciously, indeed purposely, in the bargains—but without understanding all of one's own motives or the effects of one's actions.

Take the matter of controlling a class. Many teachers dread losing control, which suggests to them a maelstrom of loud and destructive activity running on and on while the supervisor listens in the hallway. In such a situation, any alliance between teacher and student seems to the teacher to have been broken by the students. It may even seem that, before it can be reestablished, some kind of drastic action is needed to "Restore Order."

This is a good place to return to our analogy of the therapist-patient relationship. When a patient rebels against his therapist, the *last* thing a wise therapist considers is trying to get the patient back under control. The rebellion *means* something. It is not simply a hostile act, aimed at disappointing the therapist. It is a sign, to borrow concepts from still another field, that the patient senses an error and is trying to correct it: an error between his goals and his perceived reality.

It is natural, but unprofessional, for a therapist to assume the rebellion of her patient signifies some inner conflict in the patient. That *could* be true, of course. But it is possible that the patient is quite justified. The therapist may unknowingly be trying to force the patient to do, say, or be something incompatible with his present-time structure of goals. Anyone—neurotic, normal, superman—will resist efforts to push him away from his goals. Whether the patient should have different goals is beside this particular point. He resists interference or force in terms of the goals he does in fact have. The goals may not be well chosen, even for his own purposes (that is part of the neurotic problem), let alone someone else's purposes (which is a social problem).

The wise therapist, therefore, does not meet rebellion with opposition. She knows from the rebellion that in some way she is *already* viewed by the patient as an opponent. Attempts to control the rebellion would only call forth more of the same rebellion—for the same reason it began. Rather than react to the rebellion with opposition, the therapist examines the situation, first, to see whether her own attempts to satisfy her own goals are causing the problem and, second, to see how a bargain can be struck that will remove the immediate disturbance, hence restoring the long-term alliance.

The aim of therapy is to create self-awareness and insight under the modest assumption that the patient, not the therapist, needs help. In the classroom, however, unlike the clinic, both the professional problem and the behavioral problem are the teacher's problems far more than they are the students'. If the students rebel, the most reasonable assumption is that the teacher has inadvertently been creating conditions that the students see as causing discrepancies between what they want and what they experience. They are simply reacting as human beings react in such circumstances.

It is in this kind of situation that the teacher must be sensitive to systems consonance and systems conflict. The overall alliance depends on a host of subsidiary bargains—both parties to the alliance must be satisfied at *every* level. When they are so satisfied, the goal systems of both are consonant; when they are not, the goal systems are in conflict.

In reaching the overall goal of systems consonance, there is always a more or less difficult choice of more or less varied means. Sorting through those choices of means becomes, in turn, a process of selecting goals—subgoals—which in turn suggest still more detailed means. If the teacher cannot adjust her lower order goals freely, then the striking of acceptable bargains becomes impossible, and goal systems conflict becomes inevitable.

The teacher who is unwilling to examine personal goals with the idea of selecting freely among them to achieve a more general goal cannot resolve conflicts with students. Such a teacher resorts to threats and ultimately (to give the threats substance) force. When that situation is reached, the learning alliance has ceased to exist. If that situation is maintained for very long, there is no point in trying to reestablish it. The immediate conflict in present time is the only problem of any consequence to the participants in the conflicted dyad, which is all that is left of the learning alliance.

The prescription for resolution of such conflicts can be stated far more simply than it can be accomplished. Nevertheless, the prescription is the only one that will work: stop doing whatever it is that causes the conflict. For a teacher to follow such a prescription requires a depth of self-knowledge and understanding of human nature and human social relationships that is, for anyone who has not gone deeply into such areas, almost unreasonable to expect—or so it seems. Nevertheless, we think that going into these matters can be rewarding to any teacher who seeks to establish and maintain a learning alliance.

The solution to goal systems conflict is not the sort of thing that can be described as a procedure. It is a collection of attitudes— attitudes that automatically lead toward the creation of valid and satisfactory bargains, and away from a choice of subgoals that generate the conflict that endangers the alliance.

The causes of conflict—or at least the causes a teacher has the power to control—are difficult to see precisely because they are part of her goals. Whatever a teacher is doing that causes the conflict is something the teacher consciously *wants* to do. A teacher who *wants* absolute quiet in the classroom finds it constantly necessary to hush people, to speak sharply, to punish. Since the goal appears necessary as a means toward the superordinate goal of orderliness and that in turn as a means toward a yet higher goal of effective teaching, it is difficult for that teacher to see that the *need* for hushing up the class arises from the goal of achieving silence. The students, on the other hand, have made an alliance to get educated, not a bargain to keep quiet. In the absence of their making such a bargain, they naturally oppose efforts to quiet them.

The opposition of the students, who have not made the bargain to be quiet, is obviously expressed in being loud and unruly whenever the teacher calls for quiet. If more effort is made to keep them quiet, they make more effort to be noisy. Thus the very effort to make them quiet calls forth—quite automatically and naturally, for there is certainly no moral opprobrium implied here— an effort by the students in the opposite direction. Cause—and effect.

In the midst of such a situation, a teacher's attention is not likely to be on this cause-effect relationship. Rather she is searching for a means of achieving her subgoal of keeping the students quiet. She sees the resistance as a voluntary and deliberately perverse act on the part of the students, either unrelated to her superordinate goal of doing good teaching or designed to thwart it. Therefore she sees it as unrelated to her actions for, in her own view, she is acting in such a way as to make good teaching possible. The student rebellion is seen by the teacher, in short, as an act that causes a discrepancy between what the teacher *wants* to experience and what she in fact is experiencing. The teacher, just as much as the students, is rebelling. She is trying to correct an error. It is just as natural for the teacher to do this as it is for the students. Cause—and again, effect.

There is a symmetry in the situation that makes it look hopeless. And indeed it is hopeless if the teacher has no more understanding of what is happening than the students have.

Obviously, to alter such a goal systems conflict, something must undo the symmetry. Somebody must realize the way in which the attempts by one party to correct errors are causing errors in the other party. It seems reasonable to say that the teacher is, or can be, the better equipped to be that somebody. But it is unlikely that one teacher, alone, can find the point of view that will unravel the knotted relationships. A third party is needed—someone who can see where the structure of goals (both the goals of the teacher and those of the student) are stuck.

In order to stop doing what is causing the conflict, one must stop wanting something to happen. That is obvious—but it is very difficult to do. The difficulty arises because one has a *purpose* for wanting what one wants. The teacher wants silence *in order to teach effectively*. Just here, however, unanticipated results get in the way again. If the teacher stopped wanting silence, and therefore stopped trying to quiet the class, wouldn't chaos erupt? That is the commonsense prediction. It seems perfectly obvious that one's efforts to create silence have been opposing efforts clearly designed to create noise. And it would seem that if you remove the opposition, and the efforts to create noise were unchecked, then all chance of effective teaching would be gone.

However, the prediction is considerably altered if we change our point of view away from the culturally reinforced commonsense one: that is, if we see the students' efforts to make noise as being *created* by the effort to silence them. It is altered even more if it is realized that the students, too, operate with a hierarchy of their own goals. The teacher perceives an event as a disturbance that makes teaching difficult. The same event is seen by a student as communication that accomplishes some higher goal of his own. And here is where we come to the crux of bargain making.

If a person is aware that he is seeking one goal only as a means toward another, he is to that extent aware of his own goal structure. He also has hold of a possible solution to his problem. By the same token, when one sees what purpose another person's goal-directed actions achieve, he is aware (though less perfectly) of the other's goal structure. This sort of awareness is often all that is needed to resolve a conflict. It is a matter of transferring attention from symptoms to causes.

At one level, we can say that suppression directly creates rebellion, through the universal fact that people (like any other animal) resist when their goal-seeking actions are disturbed. At another level, however, we can say that the superordinate cause of the conflict is failure to recognize the purpose of seeking a given goal—that is, failing to see what would be achieved if the lower order goal were in fact accomplished. If the students were allowed to talk, what would they talk about? Too many teachers would answer that question with a stereotype, without ever finding out the answer.

If one opposes another person's goal-seeking behavior at one level, then he not only prevents attainment of that goal, but all higher order goals to which it is only a means. To repeat: when the teacher silences her class, she not only wipes out their goal to talk or make noise, but everything else that they were hoping to achieve—which incidentally meant making noise. Similarly, the teacher's highest goal—to teach well—is wiped out by the students' invalidating one of her lower goals.

The trick in successful bargain making then is to get an inkling of what the other person's higher order goals are. Then an alternative means must be offered for him to achieve them—an alternative that one finds more acceptable in terms of one's *own* goals. Only if such a bargain can be found is it possible for human beings to interact for very long without disabling conflict.

Why is such a simple-sounding resolution so difficult? There are two major reasons: first, one has to remember in the heat of conflict that the solution exists. That is very difficult when all of one's attention is captured by the search for a way to win a contest. While so intensely involved, a teacher will forget that it *is* a contest. Even if, in calmer moments, she can see that the contest was unnecessary, classroom crises are not calmer moments—crises arise in classrooms, and will continue to arise.

The second reason is more profound: it is more difficult to see how goal structures conflict if one is unaware of one's own structure of goals. And that, unfortunately, is more often the case than not. Being aware of one's ultimate goal does not automatically provide one with insights about the means one uses (and which are, therefore, intermediate goals or subgoals) to achieve the ultimate goal.

There is a direct and inescapable relationship between the teacher's self-knowledge and the teacher's ability to avoid creating conflict in the classroom. Unexamined goals are unchangeable goals. Unchangeable goals cannot be adjusted. When goals cannot be adjusted but are nevertheless interfered with, then higher order goals cannot be achieved. When one cannot choose among alternative goals freely, one cannot find or carry out the bargains that will permit a learning alliance to continue in being.

A person who could see his own structure of goals entire would be unusual indeed. A teacher embroiled in day-to-day problems has neither the leisure nor the expensive professional guidance required for such complete self-understanding. Yet it is possible to see *enough* of what is going on, a little at a time, to reach a useful understanding. One need not trace one's goals all the way to the highest or least conscious levels in order to begin to appreciate how goals can be changed and conflicts can be resolved in a way that demands *neither* winning nor giving in. If one party merely wins and the other merely gives in, the result is likely to be as wasteful a diminution of the learning alliance as the overt conflict itself.

It is normal for conflicts to arise in any group of human beings, if only because they are poorly informed about each other's intentions. What is not normal is for the conflict to persist and worsen. When conflict becomes chronic, that is a sign that some goal that ought to be adjustable has become frozen. There is nothing abnormal about the ensuing struggle, for all persons will exert energetic efforts to prevent frustration of goal achievement (even little goals like pushing open a door that is stuck shut). The cause of the *persistence* of the conflict is almost always the assumption that this goal is the *only* means or the *only acceptable* means to some higher end. Usually such assumptions are wrong. The teacher trying to communicate something to the class may have forgotten that *communication* is the goal, not *speaking,* which is only one of many means of communication. If the message is "class dismissed," what is wrong with writing it on the blackboard?

We have used the example of losing control of a class because, aside from the immediate goals such as speaking, communicating, or dismissing the class (in hierarchical order), there is often a much more fundamental and general goal at fault in conflict situations: the desire for control itself. This is indeed at the heart of the difficulties in the learning alliance because it is so seldom an overt and admitted goal. Often the superordinate goal, desire for control itself, turns out to be the "real reason" behind the choice of subgoals such as politeness, quiet, and cooperation. The goal of control is thought to be (if it is thought about at all) a means toward the even higher order goal of teaching *per se*—but that is usually a defense. If the higher order goal is teaching, then the subgoals, or means, can be adjusted. If the goal of control is not admitted or even known, then it is itself the means for creating the conflict, guaranteeing rebellion. It is the antithesis of bargain making.

To try to control the behavior of another person is to ignore the fact that his behavior is already serving *his* goals, and cannot be arbitrarily altered without frustrating the achievement of his goals. Even behaviorists who follow B. F. Skinner's recommendations have recognized that direct forceful interference is "aversive" and results in "negative reinforcement." Control through threats and direct force is recognized by all students of learning phenomena as counterproductive.

It is not so well-accepted as a fact that even *positive reinforcement or reward,* when used to achieve control, is also counterproductive. When speaking of the efficacy of reward, behaviorists tend to gloss over the step that must precede reward in order to make it most effective: deprivation of whatever is to be given as a reward. In day-to-day relationships among human beings, the *deprivation* phase of operant conditioning cannot be disguised, and takes on the appearance of punishment or deliberate withholding. When that happens, the reward becomes empty of significance, and the schedule of reinforcement is seen as arbitrary cruelty. Human beings will not put up with that situation any longer than it takes them to find a way out of it.

Despite these facts, which we think are indisputable, there are situations (even classroom situations exactly like the one we used as an example) in which reward seems extraordinarily effective and free of repercussions. When examined critically, however, these situations turn out to involve not control of behavior but the abdication of control and the substitution of bargain making.

A teacher having control problems, for example, was recently given the following advice by a good behaviorist: (1) ignore the students who are disrupting the class; and (2) reward those students who are better-behaved by showing friendliness and encouragement. "Control" returned within a week. The crux was using the proper schedule of reinforcement: give the "reward" *after* the desired behavior, rather than offering it first as a bribe.

This is not control. The teacher is bargaining to behave in a way the students find pleasant whenever the students behave in a way the teacher finds pleasant. All the teacher was in fact told to do was to express her true reactions to the behavior she appreciated, not before it happened (which would amount to an attempt to control behavior) but after the students voluntarily did anything she found pleasing. In effect, she permitted the students to see their effect on her, and she *stopped* doing all the other things that were exacerbating the conflict. She gave the students control of their perceptions of her by means of behavior acceptable to her, and found that she was then soon able to achieve her *own* goals.

This is what we mean by a bargain: creating a situation in which all parties can achieve their own goals by means that do not prevent others from achieving theirs. To create this kind of bargain requires giving up all thought of arbitrarily determining another person's behavior. It requires the willingness to broaden one's definition of acceptable behavior sufficiently to provide room for individual variations, rather than specifying one and only one behavior as acceptable. Doing this successfully may require soul-searching: "*Can* I give up control? Do I *want* students to seek their own goals?"

It is likely that in order to accept the substitution of bargain making for control, a teacher may have to undergo some inner turmoil.

It is *always* difficult to turn your worst enemy into your best tool: control of the countertransference is not easy; recognizing culture shock is not easy when you are angry and miserable. But at the end of such a process is achievement of a goal often thought of as a wistful dream—a real learning *alliance*. Good bargain making leads almost automatically to the use of the goal-systems conflict to solve itself. The teacher and the students complement and fulfill one another's goals, without overt conflict and perhaps even with affection.

Summary

When the therapeutic alliance goes wrong, the therapist asks what she did, not what the patient did. What the patient did is data.

Where the ethnographic alliance goes wrong, the ethnographer asks what she did wrong, not what the informants did wrong. What the informants did is data.

When the learning alliance goes wrong, the teacher should ask which of her subgoals is interfering with the goals of the student. We recognize that some students seem to come into the class already thoroughly programmed to disrupt—with disruption as a major goal—and that teachers have to deal with their predecessors' failures. But that very fact—combined with perfectly normal defense mechanisms—has allowed it to become culturally normal for teachers to ask "What did *he* do?" instead of "What did *I* do?"

Like the therapist and the ethnographer, the only behavior a teacher can control is her own. In order to fulfill her highest level goals, she must control her own behavior to a hierarchy of ends so that the student will find getting an education the best way to achieve his own goals.

5 | Assessing Alternative Teaching-Learning Alliances

DAVID C. EPPERSON

Any teacher who has ever solicited student opinion about the kind of teaching preferred is painfully aware of the diversity one discovers. In college classrooms, for instance, one finds counter-cultural "intimacy-freaks," who insist that the teacher *require* students to be self-disclosing and expressive. There are also self-righteous moralists, who demand that the teacher enter into an alliance with them against the evils of the Establishment. Then there are the upwardly mobile vocationally-oriented students attempting to "make it in the system," who want the teacher to be precise about what is required in making the grade. There are students experiencing the inner conflicts which accompany working through authority relations, who find it convenient to use the teacher to help them test their personal identity, calling upon the teacher to provide a supportive climate where they can try on various "masks." There are still others experiencing a nagging sense of guilt, in search of a world view that will guide them to redemption. There are those experiencing the despair of discovering that there does not appear to be a reliable belief system, who want someone to share in their dark mood. And there are even some students who have a compelling need to know— who are pleased to have the teacher engage them in conventional didactic exercises.

All of us dedicated to helping others learn can agree that students should have access to someone who can help free them from loneliness, a sense of impropriety, incompetence, inner conflict, identity diffusion, guilt, despair, ignorance, or any of the other forms of discontent. While these freedom-giving goals are shared by many, a major problem in helping learners cope with their discontent is deciding upon the type of alliance that is most likely to help them develop as fully functioning persons. All teachers have to make decisions about which forms of discontent are to become focal in relationships with learners and which teaching strategies are most likely to help learners come to terms with their personal dilemmas.

Alliances in Teaching

In this chapter, I will describe eight types of alliances that are currently being advocated by those conducting education (teachers), those receiving education (students), and those sponsoring education (parents and other citizens). In a pluralistic society, with numerous competing perspectives for ordering the complexity of human development, there is perennial debate and tension among those engaged in the planning and conduct of education. Since most of us are in agreement that a wide range of teaching-learning alliances may be legitimate, but realize that it is impossible to pursue all of them with equal vigor, our instructional decisions are made extremely difficult. In addition, many of us are divided within ourselves as to the type of alliance we feel we should attempt to establish with learners. There may also be a gap between the type of teacher we would *like* to be, and the type we are *prepared* to be. By examining a variety of types of teaching-learning alliances and the perspectives on human development upon which they are based, we may be better able to establish realistic goals for ourselves and develop the means for reconciling the competing demands we experience.

Assumptions. My scheme for examining alternative teaching-learning alliances and their attendant perspectives on human development is based upon the following set of assumptions:

1. The difficulties encountered in performing developmental tasks —that is, the tasks of developing competencies, purposes, integrity, etc.—give rise to varying degrees of discontent.*
2. At each stage in a person's development, he experiences a difficult constellation of discontents (e.g., anxiety attendant on a lack of clarity of identity in late adolescence).
3. A pervasive human motive is to get resolution on the varieties of discontent.
4. Contemporary perspectives on human development differ regarding the type of discontent that is focal (e.g., for many Marxists, it may be *a sense of impropriety*; for many counter-culturalists, *loneliness,* etc.).
5. The kind of alliance that each teacher seeks to establish with those he is attempting to educate is intimately related to the discontents focal for him at that point in *his* life.
6. The teacher's influence in alliances is dependent upon his resourcefulness in helping learners cope with their discontent.
7. The teacher's resourcefulness is intimately related to his ability to bring the realm of meaning in which he is immersed (i.e., his discipline) to bear on student discontent.

Alternative Alliances Against Discontent

Figure 1 represents eight different types of teaching-learning alliances: the Erotic, the Humanistic, the Therapeutic, the Moral, the Dogmatic, the Intellectual, the Pragmatic, and the Existential. Each type of alliance is established in order to address a particular type of learner discontent (note the outer rim of the wheel). Each type of alliance is also related to an influential perspective on human development (indicated outside the wheel). The degree to which the teacher is able to influence the learner is greatly dependent upon the

---

* The learner may or may not be able to clearly specify the nature and origins of his discontent. That is, he can experience either differentiated or undifferentiated uneasiness or dissonance in addressing his developmental tasks.

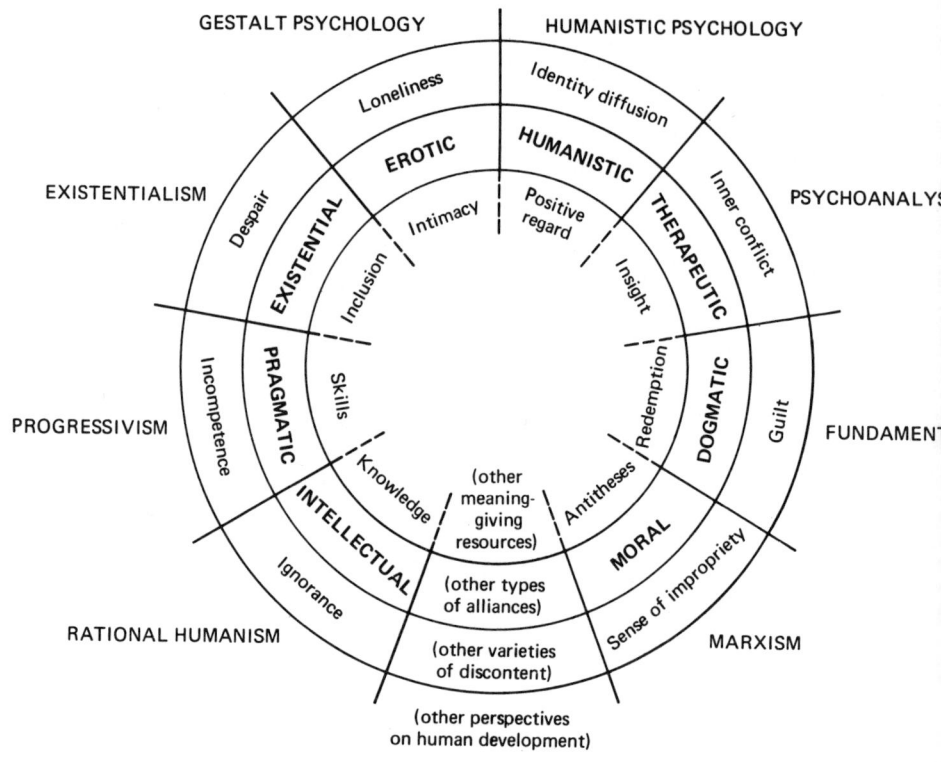

Figure 1

Teaching-Learning Alliances

Meaning-Giving Resources, Varieties of Discontent, and Perspectives on Human Development

match between the learner's felt need and the meaning-giving resourcefulness of the teacher (note the inner ring of the wheel).

It is important to point out that the alliance scheme is simply to be used as a tool for gaining an appreciation of the competing demands that exist in most teaching-learning situations. Ongoing relationships between teachers and learners are extremely complicated, with students experiencing a complex of discontents generated by the particular array of developmental tasks they are facing. At any point in time, a learner may be simultaneously attempting to deal with a number of pressing concerns. Teachers too should not be thought of as seeking to establish only one type of alliance with learners. They frequently have a number of meaning-giving resources they wish to make available to learners. However, the position taken in this chapter is that the character of teaching-learning alliances is established by the developmental tasks that have become focal for both the teacher and learner.

It seems important to acknowledge that teachers too are developing personalities, struggling with their own developmental tasks. Some teachers, for example, may still be "hung up" on a task that is customarily met and resolved at an earlier stage in most individual's development (e.g., working through authority relationships). For reasons peculiar to a teacher's personal history, he may continue to be dominated by a particular developmental task. Therefore, he may project upon his students similar concerns.

Before elaborating the different types of alliances, I would like to address a question that will inevitably be raised. How does the alliance scheme accommodate *nonrelationships,* situations in which the student "does not seem to be interested in anything"? In other words, is it realistic to assume that all students possess high enough levels of discontent to propel them into the search for growth-producing alliances? This, too, is a complicated question. While there are indeed numerous factors contributing to learner apathy, it would appear that *most* "nonrelationships" between teachers and learners can be diagnosed as mismatches between learner discontent and the resources he attributes to the teacher. It seems safe to conclude that since all growing individuals are struggling with one or another developmental task, teachers can, with most learners, find, or in some cases, even *trigger* the expression of a motive force or discontent. Whether a teacher is interested in a learner's discontent or qualified to assist him in coping with it are also important considerations.

In examining the alliance scheme then, it is necessary to keep in mind that the kinds of alliances sought and offered are generally combinations of the types described below, and that it is assumed that failures in teaching-learning relationships can often be traced to mismatches between the focal discontents of learners and the resources offered by the teacher.

Erotic Alliances. As we all know, in the process of attempting to establish satisfying interpersonal relations, each of us experiences loneliness. As individuals move from intimate relations with members of their family to more specialized and distant relationships, they are often frustrated in their efforts to establish really close personal ties. Furthermore, in recent years, there has been an effort among the more privileged in American society to seek out "peak" experiences in which they encounter themselves in new ways in the context of intimate relations with others. The human potential movement has been built, at least in part, upon the post-industrial need for establishing a sense of community with one's fellow men and has been facilitated by opportunities that contemporary affluence and leisure provide for gaining satisfaction of higher order personal needs—needs which tend to come to the forefront after the more basic needs for shelter, security, etc., have been met. Those teachers and learners experiencing a sense of "lost community" and/or a need to transcend the limits of normal interpersonal experience often demonstrate a preference for Erotic alliances.

I am using the term "erotic," not in a narrow sexual sense, but to indicate a highly personal, expressive, sometimes even sensual, emphasis in the teaching-learning situation. In Erotic alliances, the goal becomes one of putting the participants in closer touch, not only with one another, but with those unexplored and underdeveloped dimensions of self. My experiences over the past few years have indicated that there are a number of privileged youth who possess a compelling drive to enter into teaching-learning situations where they can "let it all hang out"; where teachers and learners are not "up tight"; where informality, openness, impulse expression, etc., can become the dominant features of the classroom environment. Teachers and learners who strongly feel these intimacy needs often become very impatient with those who consider the satisfaction of these needs inappropriate to the educational situation.

Gestalt psychology is one intellectual perspective upon which this approach to education has leaned. Fritz Perls and those who have elaborated and extended his views to a variety of learning contexts ranging from Esalen in Big Sur, California, to public schools, offer a theoretical perspective that can be used to justify Erotic alliances. This perspective also provides a set of meaning-giving symbols (e.g., "the here and now") to guide alliances motivated by intimacy and personal growth needs.

I do not mean to imply by the foregoing that all teachers and learners who seek out Erotic alliances are disciples of human potential theorists and practitioners. I only mean to indicate that there has emerged an intellectual perspective to give voice to the focal concerns of a good many individuals.

Humanistic Alliances. In a pluralist cultural context with both real and anticipated social mobility, with a wide range of value systems from which to choose, most individuals experience dilemmas at some point in their lives about how to define themselves. They face what is often referred to as an "identity crisis," asking: "Who am I?" or "What do I want to *be*?" To some degree, all learners face the developmental task of establishing an identity. When this need for clarifying identity becomes central for an individual, he often seeks out alliances that promise self-defining reactions from those around him. Many individuals with a high priority self-definition task become frustrated with teaching-learning situations that do not provide the kinds of nonthreatening support that will allow them to try out new ways of reacting to others. They find it difficult to achieve resolution on who they are unless provided with a climate that supports experimentation and self-exploration.

The humanistic psychology of Carl Rogers provides a perspective on human development that places a high premium on establishing nonthreatening, nurturant relationships with learners which can facilitate the development of realistic self-definitions. For Rogers, a preeminent concept which gives guidance to the teacher is "positive regard." The teacher must, according to his view, prize the uniqueness of each learner so that he can fully actualize his potential.

The guidance movement in schools and colleges is, in part, a response to the widespread need expressed by many students to get greater clarity on their identity. Rogers' theoretical perspective and the nondirective techniques he advocates have had a profound influence on the thinking of teachers as well as counselors.

Therapeutic Alliances. As we attempt to reconcile the demands of our culture and our innermost impulses and urges, we inevitably experience conflict. We often sense a need to establish alliances that provide opportunities to come to an understanding of this tension. It is not uncommon for students with nagging personal conflicts to use relationships with teachers to act out their concerns, whether or not the teachers consciously invite such responses. If, for example, the student is attempting to work through authority problems, he may transfer to the teacher the qualities of his parents and unload his mixed feelings on the teacher. As one would expect, most teachers are unprepared to accept these transference gestures. Hence, they react defensively in ways that can perpetuate the learners' inner tensions.

The psychoanalytic perspective gives the various forms of inner conflict high priority. Psychoanalytic theory calls attention to the developmental task of learning to cope effectively with feelings. Bruno Bettelheim and Richard M. Jones offer examples of the kinds of perspectives that focus upon the role of inner conflict, fantasy, and emotion in teaching-learning situations.

Dogmatic Alliances. When individuals are unable to live up to their own standards of behavior, they often are plagued by a sense of guilt. Hence, one can expect learners who have adopted standards which are difficult or impossible to live by to seek out alliances that promise a dogma that allows for "redemption." While today there appears to be relatively little interest among young people in religious dogma, there is definitely a quest by many for a clear-cut set of beliefs that will give order and meaning to their lives. The "Jesus freaks" represent one group of young people who appear to be engaged in a frantic search for redemption. Many youth attracted to this demanding fundamentalist symbol system openly seek to be redeemed from the sins of their involvement in the drug culture. While, clearly, this particular fundamentalist revival engages only a few young people, it is my view that there are many other students in quest of a system of beliefs, a dogma, that will allow them relief from guilt. Many learners enter teaching-learning situations in search of alliances with experts (or maybe, in this case, we should call them priests) who can offer solace and guidance in the learner's quest for absolution. Needless to say, there are teachers who are more than willing to take on the responsibilities of the priesthood by "laying on" a secular, if not a religious, dogma. Very often, however, those in search of redemption find that most teachers, rather than leading them to redemption, simply add to their guilt by enforcing the very standards that are the sources of their dissatisfaction with themselves.

College and university faculties are generally of little value to students in search of a comforting dogma. The prevailing ethic on most campuses is a critical analysis, which is, in effect, iconoclastic. The pervasive liberal ideology as typically presented has the effect of intensifying rather than reducing the student's guilt feelings.

The fundamentalist religious tradition, with its long history of influence in certain sectors of American society, provides a justification for Dogmatic alliances. While many academics look with scorn upon this tradition, it does offer the option of redemption that many students seek.

Moral Alliances. As young people observe the world around them, it is easy to recognize significant gaps between what *is* and what *ought to be*. Many experience a sense of impropriety and seek out alliances with others who are willing to share in their outrage. In Moral alliances, students hope to be presented with solutions to human problems that will permit the achievement of a greater correspondence between what *ought to be* and *is*.

These learners are sometimes drawn to the rhetoric of radical social and political criticism, and to iconoclastic teachers who appear to share their outrage and discontent. It should be noted that radical faculty often seek out alliances with learners in which they capitalize upon the young person's struggle for independence from family influence by ruthlessly challenging conventional belief systems. This sometimes reflects the illusion of a match between learner needs and teacher resources. The real student need may be to establish autonomy, which manifests itself in criticism of the Establishment. While it is not the purpose of this chapter to deal with the difficult problem of differentiating *real* from *illusory* matches between learner needs and teacher resources, it seems important to acknowledge the possibility of illusory matches. There are indeed cases where learner satisfaction in a Moral alliance is relatively high without any evidence of making progress on the developmental tasks that thrust him into the relationship with the teacher.

The Marxist tradition provides an intellectual justification for establishing moral alliances with learners. The appeal of the Marxist rhetoric is its emphasis upon justice and equality. Clearly, the Marxist perspective has provided contemporary social critics with powerful tools for expressing moral outrage.

Intellectual Alliances. One dimension of man's predisposition to master the world around him is reflected in his need to know. Clearly, all learners to varying degrees express this need. It does not, however, always manifest itself in a need to know what the teacher feels the learner should know! Often when students experience this type of discontent, they seek out individuals who they feel can help them reduce their ignorance. Intellectual alliances are relatively comfortable for most teachers, for their experiences and often their temperaments make them responsive to learner initiatives to increase their sense of mastery. Many, if not most, teachers would be happy if their role could be structured in such a manner that the primary types of alliances learners attempted to negotiate were intellectual in emphasis. While most statements of purposes advanced by educational policymakers place knowledge acquisition at the top of the list, the task of achieving intellectual competence becomes only *one* of many developmental tasks to which educational institutions have become committed.

Teachers have no difficulty identifying justifications for Intellectual alliances. The rational humanists—Robert Hutchins, Jacques Barzun, and others—have advocated the centrality of Intellectual alliances, making a case for limiting the functions of educational institutions to helping learners develop their capacity to engage in rational inquiry.

It seems important at this point to indicate that some teachers, while acknowledging that their primary responsibility is to establish effective Intellectual alliances, enter into other types of alliances as means for creating rapport and/or in recognition that it is not possible to promote intellectual competency without attending to other dimensions of learner development. In other words, they can justify entering into other types of alliances if it can be demonstrated that they will serve as means to the ultimate end of education, the development of the ability to conduct rational inquiry into fundamental human problems.

Pragmatic Alliances. For most people, a pervasive reason for becoming educated is to gain skills that will lead to rewards and recognition. The sense of incompetence, both vocational and social, that many learners experience is what propels them toward establishing Pragmatic alliances. The centrality of Pragmatic alliances is especially evident among those learners from lower and middle income groups who approach education primarily as a vehicle for social mobility. The influx into the American educational system of large numbers of individuals from less economically advantaged backgrounds has led to the development of more practical learning options, where the teacher's role becomes one of serving as a resource to help learners develop specific marketable skills (witness the junior college movement). In many cases, it is no longer sufficient for the teacher to help the learner develop only conceptual knowledge, he must also help him develop his practical problem-solving skills. In some cases, he is even expected to help the learner develop human relations skills that can facilitate practical social functioning.

This problem-solving emphasis has its roots in the progressivist tradition as articulated by John Dewey and his followers. The progressivist perspective has provided a justification for educational arrangements that make practical applications a first order of business. Some of our educational institutions, especially elite colleges and universities, have resisted vigorously policies that promote these types of teaching-learning alliances.

Existential Alliances. With the many competing value systems available, the task of establishing personal purposes and direction has been made extremely difficult. Frequently, in attempting to determine which goals are worth pursuing, learners are sent into a state of despair.

It is indeed difficult to suffer this despair alone. Both teachers and learners experiencing these feelings of purposelessness often attempt to share their concerns in the hope of discovering something in which they can believe.

The existential philosopher, Martin Buber, has addressed this concern, as have numerous other philosophers, writers, and artists. The existentialists provide a perspective which articulates the need for alliances that aid the learner in his search for purpose and meaning. (Buber advocates what he calls *inclusive* relationships.)

It has not been my intention in offering this alliance scheme to attempt to be all-encompassing. Clearly, other types of alliances can be identified and related to developmental tasks—giving teachers other resources and perspectives on human development. My purpose has been simply to articulate a range of competing demands that are being made in teaching-learning situations, demands which those of us who teach experience in one form or another in our day-to-day interactions with learners and teacher colleagues.

Test of Usefulness

To test the potential utility of the scheme, let's turn our attention to some major kinds of conflicts the scheme can help us articulate.

For purposes of illustrating some potential conflicts suggested by the conceptual scheme, I have selected three types of alliances—Erotic, Moral, and Pragmatic—which focus upon quite different developmental tasks : freeing interpersonal relations, developing integrity, and developing competency, respectively. I have chosen these alliances from among the eight for several reasons : (1) they emphasize those aspects of development that most young people today experience with considerable intensity; (2) there are clearly identifiable groups of learners and teachers who employ in educational debate the arguments of the perspectives upon which these kinds of alliances are based; and (3) many classroom tensions and conflicts can be understood as resulting from the competition among these developmental forces.

To illustrate that these alliances are more than abstractions that grow out of an analysis of alternative theoretical perspectives, I would like to describe three students in my recent experience, each of whom appears to have been possessed by one of these developmental tasks almost to the exclusion of others.

First was the earnest freshman who attempted to encourage, persuade, even cajole the teacher and his classmates into turning each class meeting into an encounter group session. He was adamant in his claim that it was not ideas or technical skills that were important; instead, he insisted, we were in need of "facilitating our growth as *persons.*" He became extremely impatient with those students with clearly circumscribed skill-oriented interests in the class. More often than not, it was impossible for him to establish rapport with his classmates, except for those few confederates who shared his desire for a more intimate, informal, open, and expressive classroom environment.

Then there was the cynical sophomore who achieved his greatest satisfaction when he could engage the teacher and his classmates in radical criticism of the university and other social institutions. He became impatient and sarcastic with those classmates who defended "freaking out" with drugs, rock music, communal experiments, or encounter group experiences. While he tried to be respectful of the students from less privileged social backgrounds, many of whom wished to establish very pragmatic relationships with the teacher, his avowed rejection of conventional routes to achievement in the "system" showed through.

And finally, there was the conscientious student from a white ethnic working-class background who made every effort to derive practical applications from his classroom learnings. He worked hard at developing a relationship with the teacher that would provide access to learning resources and point to appropriate models of behavior for achieving social mobility. He was genuinely friendly, respectful, at times even deferent. He displayed an interest in social criticism as long as the discussion led to a productive search for viable alternatives. He was also curious to find out about the possibilities and limitations of personal growth approaches to education, not so much as a vehicle for achieving self-awenesss, but more to assess their potential utility in "real life" situations for promoting acquisition of subject matter. (He was a teacher trainee.)

Without question, the focal developmental tasks for these three students were quite different.

What kinds of matches and mismatches between teaching style and learner needs might one expect for different types of students? One way to approach the question is to examine how different students might respond to the various ways in which teaching functions are performed by teachers as they employ styles based upon alternative perspectives on human development. All teachers have to (1) establish limits; (2) create rapport; (3) transmit information; (4) elicit responses; (5) react to learner performance; and (6) solicit assessments from students on how their relationship is progressing. Each teaching-learning perspective suggests how these various functions might be performed. One way to anticipate how effective a match between a learner's needs and a teaching style will be (that is, whether a viable alliance can be established) is to examine how each perspective on human development would suggest that teaching functions be performed and then anticipate how a particular type of student might respond to the teacher's behavior. For example, each perspective suggests what kinds of limits the teacher should establish in relationships with learners—that is, how informal, democratic, self-disclosing, etc., he should be. By knowing how a teacher is attempting to establish limits with learners, we can anticipate how students with various focal developmental tasks will respond to the teacher's behavior. In other words, in every teaching-learning alliance, basic teaching functions need to be performed. In alliances based upon different perspectives, the functions are performed somewhat differently. It is the way in which these functions are performed that gives distinctive character to relationships based upon the various perspectives.

While it is beyond the scope of this chapter to develop a comprehensive taxonomy of teaching functions and compare each major perspective in relation to how it indicates these functions should be performed, I would like to illustrate the outcomes of such an undertaking for the three example alliances: Erotic, Moral, and Pragmatic.

Let's examine how direct experience (in contrast to abstract or second-hand experience) might be used to get information to students. In an Erotic alliance, the teacher typically makes available to the learning group a number of awareness-expanding exercises. These exercises structure to a considerable extent the kinds of experience a learner can have. In a Moral alliance, on the other hand, it could be considered important for learners to confront directly social and political ills. The teacher might make use of field trips to observe social crises directly in an effort to raise the student's consciousness of inequality and injustice. Finally, in a Pragmatic alliance, the teacher would attempt to put the learner in touch with day-to-day practical problems that could serve to generate an interest in acquiring basic knowledge and skills. He would more than likely also make use of the planning and evaluation of projects as a means for helping learners develop democratic group problem-solving skills.

In Erotic alliances, direct experience is used to put the individual in touch with his own feelings and the feelings of others; in Moral alliances, to raise consciousness and suggest alternative social and political arrangements; and in Pragmatic alliances, to promote the development of problem-solving skills. In all three cases, the perspective upon which the alliance is based dictates the use of direct experience as a means of promoting student growth. All three perspectives, in this respect, call for radical departures from traditional teaching methods.

By now, it should be clear that there is indeed a good chance in most educational settings for a mismatch between student needs and teacher style. If teachers attempt to establish alliances which place high priority on developmental tasks that are of little concern to students, one can expect difficulty in establishing a growth-producing relationship. When one acknowledges that most educators are primarily trained to establish intellectual alliances (and one might conclude, not very well trained at that), it is not difficult to understand why there are so many learners in our educational system who sense a mismatch between their needs and the resources offered by teachers. We can expect that the three students described earlier would have some difficulty adapting to the approaches of most teachers in our educational system.

The process of matching learner needs and teacher resources is made difficult by still another reality of interpersonal relations. A teacher cannot simply announce what resources he has available; he must both display in an attractive way what he can offer learners *and* develop learner trust before a viable relationship can be established. While acknowledging that these two functions are crucial to establishing and maintaining effective teaching-learning alliances, it is beyond the scope of this chapter to deal with them in the detail they deserve. However, it is necessary to understand that until these two functions are effectively performed, it is impossible for alliances to be established.

It is no wonder that educational innovators who attempt to break the conventional mold by offering to enter into nontraditional types of alliances with learners frequently meet resistance and become frustrated and eventually cynical. It is difficult for many radical educators to accept student rejection of approaches they consider crucial to personal and social development. It is easy to be angered by "ungrateful," "unresponsive" rebuffs of genuine efforts to facilitate student development and to right social wrongs.

Another problem for advocates of nontraditional approaches is whether any society is prepared to invest in the training of teachers to enter into these demanding types of alliances. Clearly, most teachers are underprepared to establish even conventional Intellectual alliances. Imagine the tremendous costs of training a cadre of teachers to establish Therapeutic alliances, for example. Our society gives little evidence of being eager to even maintain its present level of investment in teacher education. This, of course, is a problem of social policy and must be addressed by those engaged in decision making at that level. But where does all of this leave the harried classroom teacher who is faced with the daily task of performing teaching functions, with the challenge of selecting from among the range of alternative perspectives an approach from which he can gain some measure of satisfaction? In the final section of the chapter, I will address the question of how one might go about assessing the appropriateness of alternative perspectives on human development.

Criteria for Evaluating Alternative Perspectives

One might conclude from the foregoing that each perspective on human development is as valid as the other, depending upon what one is attempting to accomplish in a teacher-learning relationship. For example, it could be argued that if one is attempting to help a learner develop his spelling ability, a Pragmatic alliance is in order, hence a perspective such as B. F. Skinner's should be evoked. Or, if one is attempting to help a student increase his self-confidence, a Humanistic alliance as proposed by Rogers might be considered most appropriate. A bag of tricks approach to teaching-learning alliances which concludes that "it depends upon the aims of the relationship or the types of student needs," ignores that the selection of aims or the identification of student needs both require a perspective, a system for determining priorities. We all recognize loneliness, injustice, guilt, etc., as widespread human discontents; but each of us has to decide which of these should receive immediate attention. Unless one is prepared to accept a naive view of cultural relativism in which one rejects the possibility of identifying the means for evaluating alternative points of view or is willing to adopt an oversimplified, hopeless, psychological determinism, it is necessary to conclude that teachers can and should weigh a range of alternative perspectives before choosing a point of view to guide their teaching decisions. I would therefore like to propose some criteria that seem appropriate for evaluating perspectives on human development:

1. *Quality of Outcomes*
    a. *Do alliances based upon the perspective result in the learner's increased ability to cope with his discontent?*
    b. *Do alliances based upon the perspective result in the teacher's increased ability both to cope with his discontent and to facilitate learner growth?*

Clearly, the single most important criterion in judging a perspective has to be whether the participants in teaching-learning alliances based upon the perspective benefit from the relationship. If there are few enduring benefits—as has been demonstrated in many of the follow-up studies on teaching, therapy, and sensitivity training—then the perspective needs to be reassessed.

Many perspectives fail to recognize the social benefits of maximizing teacher development both in their fields of inquiry and as facilitators of student learning. Teacher outcomes cannot be ignored if one is concerned about the enduring effects of educational policies.

2. *Scope of Needs Addressed*
   a. *Does the perspective provide for accommodating a wide range of learner needs?*
   b. *Does the perspective provide for accommodating a wide range of teacher needs?*

A perspective which assists in addressing a wide range of student needs has significant advantages, especially in a rapidly changing pluralistic society. A perspective which also has the flexibility of accommodating a range of teacher intellectual and emotional needs is also advantageous.

3. *Establishing Priorities*
   a. *Does the perspective establish a clear system of priorities regarding the types of discontent that should be addressed?*
   b. *Does the perspective advance an approach to reconciling competing demands (either between learners or between the teacher and learners)?*

An interpersonal *perspective,* in contrast to a *theory* of interpersonal behavior, must provide a basis for determining learning objectives. A teacher is not simply a social engineer carrying out a standard public mandate, but instead is responsible for selecting within rather broad limits those discontents and dilemmas he deems most important. A perspective on human development should assist him in determining which of the competing sets of values should have priority.

4. *Clarity of Instructional Imperatives*
   a. *Does the perspective provide clear imperatives regarding how teaching functions should be performed?*

Often when one is presented with a teaching-learning perspective, he is engaged by appealing rhetoric only to discover when he attempts to put the point of view into practice that its imperatives for performing basic teaching functions are too vague to be of use.

5. Scope of Instructional Imperatives

  a. *Does the perspective provide a comprehensive set of imperatives for performing teaching functions?*

For a perspective to be of real value to a practitioner, it must help him determine how to set limits, create rapport, give information, get responses, give and get feedback. Many writers in their efforts to avoid being prescriptive offer broad guidelines for practice, but fail to be comprehensive in their recommendations. They may spell out how to create rapport with students but give little or no attention to how to get information to them.

6. Acknowledgment of Reality Dimensions

  a. *Does the perspective acknowledge the limitations of educational alliances in effecting personal and social change?*

One impressive feature of the research results on personal and social change is the rather universal resistance individuals and groups offer to changing their ways. If a perspective is to be useful, it should point to these sources of resistance so that teachers can establish realistic levels of aspiration. Some of the perspectives promise too much, and hence condemn the teacher to a sense of failure when ambitious change goals are not reached.

  b. *Does the perspective clearly acknowledge the socio-political implications of alliances based upon its principles?*

Some perspectives are so psychological that they make no significant provisions for the social and political context in which alliances are established. Teaching-learning relationships occur in a dynamic socio-political arena and cannot be assessed without considering the impact of the context on alliances *and* the effect of alliances on the context.

  c. *Is the perspective parsimonious enough to be of utility to teaching practitioners?*

Clearly, teaching relationships are extremely complex social and psychological phenomena. If one is attempting to achieve a comprehensive view that accommodates a large number of contingencies, an elaborate perspective is in order. However, the practitioner has significant limitations in how many factors he can take into consideration at each point in making instructional decisions. Therefore, it may indeed be necessary to discard an elaborate and elegant perspective which seems to accommodate many contingencies in favor of one that is less elegant, on the grounds that the former is too unwieldy.

> d. *Does the perspective make provisions for the limitations the teacher's ability and character impose upon the relationship?*

Too often theorists assume that it will be possible to identify gifted practitioners who are flexible enough to respond nimbly to the many contingencies that arise in applying their approach to teaching. In fact, teachers, like all other human beings, can only be expected to adapt to a limited range of circumstances. If, indeed, a perspective is going to be useful, it should have the flexibility to accommodate teachers of diverse ability and character.

> e. *Does the perspective suggest the need for the teacher to achieve self-awareness so that he can know why he is responding as he is?*

Mindless following of the prescriptions of a perspective is not what most theorists have in mind. If a perspective is to be of value to practitioners, provisions should be made that encourage users to come to a recognition of how their character affects the way they choose to implement the perspective.

These are indeed stringent criteria for evaluating alternative perspectives. Many perspectives fail to (1) generate teaching practices that actually produce the outcome sought; (2) contain provisions that allow for the accommodation of a wide range of learner and teacher needs; (3) advance an explicit hierarchy of priorities or offer arrangements for reconciling competing values; (4) advance *precise* imperatives as to how the various teaching functions should be performed; (5) provide a comprehensive set of imperatives for performing basic teaching functions; and (6) acknowledge critical social and personal constraints and consequences of teaching-learning alliances.

An assumption that has been made in this chapter is that the way a teacher chooses to perform his teaching functions reflects his total world view: his religion, his politics, his personal history, his hang-ups, his whole person. Teaching decisions reflect an interpersonal perspective, sometimes well thought out, but more often than not an unexamined, piecemeal set of beliefs that cluster around some key emotionally meaningful symbols (e.g., "feedback," "self-actualization," "dialogue").

All educational practitioners require at least a few powerful symbols to serve and comfort them in the face of complex teaching-learning decisions. Hopefully, opportunities arise in the careers of each practitioner to reexamine the symbols which have put meaning into relationships with students. The model I have advanced with its taxonomy of alliances and its criteria for assessing alternative perspectives on human development may prove useful to those wishing to (1) consider alternative ways of approaching relationships with students; (2) develop more satisfying and effective means of performing basic teaching functions; and (3) select a personal perspective after carefully weighing its possibilities and limitations.

As long as we live in a pluralistic society with a range of emotionally charged symbols around which educators, students, and sponsors rally, we can expect perennial tension among those holding competing perspectives. While it would be comforting to settle upon clear prescriptions for guiding our teaching decisions, it is likely that every serious practitioner will be challenged from time to time to reexamine his symbol system and the assumptions upon which he is basing his relations with learners. Hopefully, the model presented in this chapter will be useful to those in search of a viable alternative for deciding how they should proceed to help learners cope with the discontents and constraints inherent in their personal situations.

6 | Influence of Individual Differences on Instructional Theories

DOLORES E. CROSS and EMILYE FIELDS

Instructional theories, and the classroom processes and structures they support, are influenced by teacher and pupil knowledge of and response to individual differences. What is more, how one teaches and responds in a given situation will depend on how participants (teacher and pupil) perceive self and others, as well as on the values they ascribe to individual differences. In an important sense, theories and tactics of teaching prove their value by the contributions they make to understanding the uniquenesses that individual learners present. A goal of this chapter is to offer a range of instructional or interactional techniques that can be utilized in responding to individuality of participants in a learning situation. Here, teachers and pupils are viewed as participants in the learning situation who possess differences in values and knowledge—as well as perceptions and reactions to differences—that are as unique as each person.

As employed in this chapter, "individual differences" refer to those mental abilities, physical characteristics, personality traits, cultural backgrounds, interests, motivations, behavioral and response mechanisms that make each person unique. What we are concerned about is the extent to which participants in the learning situation identify such differences and the manner in which they respond to them when planning and carrying out instruction. A teacher may, for example, assume that all students of a given age are pretty much alike, have identical goals, and learn at a uniform rate. If so, the interactional process will aim to make all achieve the same goals within prescribed time intervals, with no provisions being made to adapt to individual differences. In contrast, a teacher who considers individual differences as vital factors in learning will plan instruction to fit the differences that exist. Similarly, a pupil's response to other participants can reflect the individual's perception of the class as homogeneous or heterogeneous.

A goal of education for the younger learner is to achieve fundamental competencies. The students are expected to learn to read, spell, write, compute, reason, think reflectively, and master certain information about their society and its development. The goal of education of older children is extended to include proficiency in a discipline or professional field. While these goals are fairly uniform, student ability and reaction to expectations and potentialities is not uniform but contingent upon individual differences. Thus the process of completing the goals of education should begin with teacher and pupil realization of the uniqueness of participants in the situation, and in actualizing the goal the teacher should draw from a variety of instructional theories. In a circular process individual differences contribute to the development and evaluation of instructional theories, while theories augment what is known about the learner. Consequently, adaption of instruction to individual differences is vital, if all participants (educators and students) are to grow.

Certain individual differences are coming to be viewed as precious resources to be nurtured. Creative potentialities, aesthetic interests, social sensitivity, humanistic commitments may all be examples of such. Likewise, ethnic, racial, and language backgrounds—as well as other cultural characteristics—are teaching and learning resources. Individual interests, life and vocational goals are similar resources. And, of course, physical appearance and the intermix of responses that are called personality represent other categories of differences that give uniqueness to individuals. With such differences, the task of instruction is to cultivate their expression and thereby increase their benefits to the individual and society.

The intent of this chapter is to contribute to an understanding of the rationale for responding to individual differences and to highlight specific characteristics of interpersonal techniques used to respond to individual differences. Within the umbrella of this book, *Theories for Teaching*, this chapter asserts that the reality of uniqueness of participants in the learning situation contributes to the utilization and modification of instructional theories as resources in the interactional-learning process.

Reality of Individual Differences

The reality of individual differences is validated by subjective and objective data. Depending upon the nature and intensity of their experiences, individuals have different knowledge, value orientation, and repertoire of responses for reacting to individual uniqueness. Individuals differ in many ways, and subjective and objective data regarding differences can be identified and quantified. Powell suggests that there are four basic characteristics of individual differences: normality, variation, covariation, and velocity. Normality refers to the individual's position relative to normal probability on the bell-shaped curve. Variation refers to the deviations among the members of any species of living organism. Covariation refers to the interaction and interrelation of traits and ability. Velocity refers to the individual's rate of development.[1]

Comparative Knowledge

Participants enter learning situations having developed and stored unique ideas about the quality, quantity, and import of individual differences. Through formal training and the use of evidence from psychological, achievement, and ability tests, teachers have objective data on the variability of students. The data can be refined to yield a test profile indicating information on the intravariability of the individual. For example, two students who have attained the same total score may present different aptitude profiles when their performances along specific lines are analyzed. In addition to this objective data, teachers have the resources of their personal and professional experiences, which provide subjective data on human variability.

Pupils have less sophisticated data to describe differences. Through socialization, the process of social learning, the student compares self

---

[1] W. Powell, "The Nature of Individual Differences," *Organizing for Individual Differences* (Newark, Del.: International Reading Association, 1968).

and others; finds a personal social role; gives it definition; and develops it. In the early years the behavior of the young child is largely influenced by parents. Gradually during the elementary school years—and more markedly through junior and senior high school—the peer culture becomes a significant socializing agent. The student's knowledge of individual difference is largely a product of subjective data.

Thus, teachers and individual students have opportunities and dispositions for varieties of experiences that would place them at different points on a hypothetical continuum with points indicating optimal to minimal knowledge of individual differences.

Perceived Values

In addition to comparative knowledge, each participant also places a unique valuing on the differences perceived. As expressed by Cantril, perceiving is always done by a particular person from a unique position in space and time and with a personal combination of needs.[2] Valuing prompts the person to make choices. In the act of choosing, values are demonstrated. As stated by Morris: "once he chooses, something new is brought into existence: a 'way of responding to that situation. . . . In the final act, he was the one who responded and he, therefore, was the one who brought a value into being in that situation'." [3]

Assigning a positive value to individual differences could flow from philosophical, educational-psychological, and political viewpoints. The philosophy of existentialism emphatically suggests the responsibility of the individual to be aware of self and be responsible for answerability.

> A youngster who becomes full aware of himself as the shaper of his own life, aware of the fact that he must take charge of that life and make it his own statement of what a human being ought to be—this is the individual who has been brought beyond mere intellectual discipline, beyond mere subject matter, beyond mere enculturation, beyond mere

---

[2] H. Cantril and W. Ittelson, *Perception: A Transactional Approach* (New York: Doubleday and Company, 1954).

[3] Van Cleve Morris, *Existentialism in Education* (New York: Harper and Row, 1966).

"fundamental dispositions," to the exotic but supremely human zone . . . of value creation where selves create their own selves beyond the reach of teacher and textbook.[4]

The charge of existentialism is to value individual differences and be responsible for knowing and growing. The position of educational-psychologist Carl Rogers reflects a similar valuing in describing teacher qualities that permit self-directed, student selection of goals, and a style that reacts to cognitive and affective differences.[5]

Social Demands

The recognition and acceptance of the view that the United States can no longer afford the uneducated man is a key reason to choose to respond to individual differences. In a large part of the world, the worker no longer predominantly performs human tasks imposed by a pretechnological era. To prepare for the automated complexity of the twentieth-century society, he has need for the skills of the knowledgeable technician with distinctly individualized abilities and for carefully cultivated individual potential.[6] Dewey observed: "A progressive society counts individual variations as precious since it finds in them the means of its own growth. Hence, a democratic society must in consistency with its ideals allow for intellectual freedom and the play of diverse gifts and interests in the educational measures."[7]

Divergent Responses

For philosophical, educational, political, or social reasons, participants in the learning situation might endorse the value that individual differences should be respected. Conversely, there might be considerable divergence among participants as to whether there *should* be a response to individual differences—and, more specifically, dis-

---

[4] *Ibid.*, p. 48.
[5] Carl Rogers, *Freedom to Learn* (Columbus, Ohio: C. E. Merrill Publishing Company, 1969).
[6] Harold G. Shane, "The School and Individual Differences," *Individualizing Instruction,* NSSE Yearbook, Part 1 (Chicago: NSSE, 1962), pp. 44–61.
[7] J. Dewey, *Democracy and Education* (New York: The Macmillan Company, 1916), p. 357.

agreement as to which aspect of human variability should have priority. For example, a teacher might view academic mastery of geography as a valued choice, while students might view knowledge of ethnic cultures as a more valued choice.

However, few educators would deny the reality of individual differences and human variability. In a literal sense, everyone is exceptional; for although classifications are possible with respect to a given aspect of individuality and although there is a concentration of cases about the central tendency in a given trait, it is the integration of numerous and varied characteristics that gives a person individuality —and the psychological fallacy of undifferentiated or mass education, as Freeman pointed out in 1934, is apparent.[8] The question for many educators therefore is how best to respond to individual differences in the classroom structure.

Individualized Classroom Structures

The teacher initiates and maintains a particular classroom structure. Structure is defined as the general setup and resources of the room with its work/interest areas and traffic patterns. The structure can be classified as highly individualized, moderately individualized, or minimally individualized. The resources and normative behavior determine classification. A highly individualized structure is characterized by the presence of multilevel teacher and student resources; intra-classroom grouping with varying size, and purpose; differentiated assignments that are varied, challenging, and purposeful; and evidence of the exercise of teacher and pupil autonomy—characterized by pupil-teacher planning, self-selection, evaluation, and mutual assistance. The following are examples of highly individualized, moderately individualized, and minimally individualized classroom structures.[9]

[8] F. S. Freeman, *Individual Differences* (New York: Holt and Company, 1934).
[9] Ben M. Harris and Betty Coody, *Profile of Individualization of Instruction*. Instructional Leadership Training Materials, University of Texas at Austin. Revised 1971. Copyright, all rights reserved.

Profile of Individualization of Instruction

	Highly Individualized	Moderately Individualized	Minimally Individualized
Materials used are at different levels of difficulty.	All pupils work with materials that reflect different levels of difficulty.	Nearly half the pupils use materials reflecting several different levels of difficulty.	All pupils use the same materials.
Pupils work independently in intra-class groups.	Pupils work in small groups with little direction for prolonged periods of time.	Most pupils work independently in small groups for short periods of time.	Pupils work in small or large groups under the direction of the teacher at all times.
Intra-class groups vary in size and number to reflect pupil needs.	Groups range from one person to as much as half the class.	Groups vary in size, but only two or three groups are employed.	No intra-class grouping is employed.
A variety of assignments is made to individuals and small groups.	Identical assignments are given to only small groups.	Identical assignments are given to all of the class only occasionally.	All pupils are given identical assignments most of the time.

Revival of Commitment

Efforts to individualize are not new. What is happening today might better be described as a revival. As early as the seventeenth century, attempts were made to individualize instruction. Nila Bantun Smith described the Dame School of that century: "There was no particular philosophy or psychology which guided Dame School practice. The pupils who came to the Dame School were at different stages of development . . . and there was no particular need for attempting to mold them into one achievement level for mass production purposes."[10]

Many authors have discussed individualizing a structure in terms of new concepts of class organization, provision of multilevel and multi-interest resources, and expectations of self-selection and self-pacing. The terms "self-seeking," "self-direction," and "self-pacing" are outgrowths of Willard Olson's studies on child behavior. Olson endorses the child's innate potential for goal patterning, which relates to dimensions of velocity basic to individual differences.[11] Savetsky has called attention to the resources in the total environment open to the teacher who individualizes the instruction of mathematics, suggesting ways to proceed beyond the text to awareness of the geometrical aspects of nature's creations.[12] Veatch reported, in 1964, a change in children's attitude toward reading when self-selection was employed.[13] Interest in new ways to individualize instruction has also been increased by the building of large stocks of programmed materials, development of multimedia centers, use of computer-assisted programs, and introduction of more flexible time schedules.

Influencing Factors

The classroom is a structure within a series of structures. The setting can be affected by the organization of the school (as nongraded, for instance), and by the value placed on such a structure by administrators. Anderson has listed two dimensions of nongradedness that are helpful in understanding the external facilitator of classroom structure. They are (1) the philosophy (value system) that guides the behavior of the school toward the pupils; and (2) the administrative

[10] N. B. Smith, *Reading Instruction for Today's Children* (Englewood Cliffs, N.J.: Prentice-Hall, 1963), pp. 130–133.
[11] Willard C. Olson, *Child Development* (Boston: Heath and Company, 1964).
[12] M. Savetsky, "Reaching the Individual as a Person," *Individualizing Education* (Washington, D.C.: Association for Childhood Education International, 1964), pp. 37–47.
[13] J. Veatch, "Meeting Individual Differences in Reading," *Individualizing Education* (Washington, D.C.: Association for Childhood Education International, 1964).

or organizational machinery and procedure whereby the life of the pupils and teachers are regulated and facilitated.[14]

The value system of educational leaders is reflected to the extent that some things are cherished and other things are opposed. If educational leaders value independent learning by students, they will fix priorities and activate resources to ensure optimal individualization of the classroom structure. The teacher's attempt to individualize the classroom can therefore be facilitated by organizational machinery which is based on the idea of continuous progress without inhibitors of grade designations.

Conceptually, a nongraded school with multi-age, multi-achievement of grouping within classes and highly individualized classroom structure recognizes individual values and expects individual differences. *However, the degrees to which individual differences are responded to are determined by the interactional process of teacher-student, teacher-students, student-student, and student-students.* (The interactional process refers to verbal and nonverbal communication and the exercise of autonomy by participants—teacher and pupils—in the learning situation.) The heterogeneous quality of the participants implies that they enter a situation with differing knowledge and priorities. The educator's task begins with assessing knowledges and values, and with initiating and reinforcing ideas of appropriate behavior. At the same time, the student is determining what the expectations of the situation will be. If the participants are more alike than different in their knowledge and valuing of individual differences (that would place them at a relatively high point on a hypothetical continuum of optimal to low knowledge and valuing of individual differences), the following would be expected:

1. The interactional process would promote a responding to individual differences among participants.
2. The teacher could initiate and maintain a structure that could be described as highly individualized, in which there might be a significantly high response to individual differences.

[14] R. Anderson, "The Nongraded School: An Overview," *National Elementary Principals* (January, 1968), pp. 4–11.

3. The interactional process in the classroom that tolerates and expects a wide range of behaviors promotes improved knowledge and valuing of individual differences.

If there is a lack of congruence—as characterized by the teacher placing a high value on individual differences and the pupils tending toward the opposite end of the continuum—the teacher might initiate a structure that is moderately individualized and cultivate appreciation for differences through the curriculum emphasis and a supportive instructional style. In such an instance, despite this teacher's goal of optimal response to individual difference, knowledge and valuing of individual differences would have to be cultivated among the pupils. In goal setting, in order to move from one point to another on a continuum from low to high response to individual differences, the teacher should make full use of such resources as student personalities, resources in the classroom, and pupil variability in knowledge and appreciation of differences. The teacher's behavior in accepting a wide range or variation of behavior in the classroom creates a model for the students to follow. As students accept the teacher's model, they provide models for each other. As Fox has observed, the student in the classroom gets an idea of self and others in the classroom from the teacher and peers.[15]

Conversely, the teacher can be found in a situation in which the other participants, through subjective and objective experiences, know and appreciate differences better than does the teacher. If such a teacher imposes a restrictive atmosphere because of an acceptance and expectation of narrow range of behavior, the following would be expected:

1. The interactional process would retard responding to individual differences among participants.
2. The teacher could initiate and maintain a structure that could be described as minimally individualized, in which there would be significantly low response to individual differences.

[15] R. S. Fox, M. B. Luszki, and R. Schmuch, *Diagnosing Classroom Learning Environments* (Chicago: Science Research Associates, 1966).

3. The interactional process in a classroom that does not tolerate and expect a narrow range of behaviors interferes with growth of knowledge and valuing of individual differences.

In practice a teacher will not find all class members at any one point of the continuum from high to low knowledge and valuing of individual differences. For example, a teacher can have a segment of the class which is not ready for a highly individualized structure. In responding to these differences, some students could be placed with another teacher whose structure might better accommodate the needs of the students.[16] Another procedure would provide for an intra-class grouping in which the activities of this particular group of students would be largely teacher directed, and would cultivate development of knowledges and valuing of differences in a supportive atmosphere in which the teacher demonstrates that uniqueness is both expected and accepted.

Role of Teacher

It is the teacher's responsibility to structure the environment in the best possible way to help each child's interest and needs. In observing the child on a day-by-day basis, a teacher can evaluate a child's relationship with both students and adults, including the student's ability to handle frustrations that occur. The teacher's evaluation and classification of behavior is related to the classroom norms initiated by this approach. By demonstrating traffic patterns, structuring differing areas of interest, and devising resources that facilitate creativity, the teacher facilitates pupil autonomy. The care and time given to assessing and follow-up implies that differences can be objectively and subjectively perceived. In the process of this helping contact in the classroom, the individual develops in knowledge and valuing of

---

[16] Lewin Herbert Thelen, University of Chicago, attempted to take into consideration the characteristics of both teachers and pupils as they interact in the classroom. His findings indicate that, with suitable help, teachers are able to identify the kinds of students with which they are most and least successful.

In a recent study, the author (D. Cross) found that teachers who were moderately individualized, experienced greater success with children that had been identified as being significant management problems to classroom teachers.

individual differences. Thus, the classroom participants enter with varying knowledge and value orientation of individual differences. The interactional process characterized by contacts through assessing, prescribing, and instructing can lead to improved awareness of self and others, as well as to a *valuing of the differences.*

The reality of individual differences also suggests that every participant in a classroom influences the quality of organization by the extent to which he or she responds and cares about individuality. Consequently, educational leaders, colleagues, and teacher trainers have the responsibility of facilitating teacher autonomy in creating an appropriate atmosphere in which respecting, accepting, and expecting teacher variability are essential. The teacher should not be perceived as "good" or "bad" based on the structure initiated. The judgment must be based instead on whether the structure initiated is appropriate for learning of participants (after some assessment of the situation), rather than according to the lockstep of a fixed concept of the ideal environment. If the teacher's behavior retards new learning—retraining, expansion of resources, and/or reorganization should be utilized to modify her teaching style so that more adequate response to individual differences is facilitated.

The personal qualities of the teacher must be seen as one of the many variables that contribute to optimal learning—to a view where the individual teacher asks of self *not* "Do I possess the 'proper' psychological and pedagogical virtues?" but rather "What kind of person am I and how may I make the most of my uniqueness in helping children to learn?"

Carl Rogers suggests certain teacher characteristics that facilitate awareness—namely, empathy, trust, acceptance, and regard.[17] Similarly, Warren G. Bennis lists four qualities concerned with extension of identity or self-image: (1) self-realization—implies both knowing and making real or concrete; (2) selflessness—being sure enough of self-worth as an individual and being able to respond unselfconsciously; (3) facilitating relationships best defined as trust relation-

---

[17] C. R. Rogers, "What Psychology Has to Offer to Teacher Education," *Mental Health and Teacher Education,* 46th Yearbook (The Association for Student Teaching, 1967), pp. 37–57.

ships; and (4) providing descriptive feedback to the descriptive cues that can help them discover *what* they are, rather than just how acceptable they are.[18]

There is nothing new in use of multilevel material, differentiated assignments, and intra-grouping. They have been employed in varying degrees throughout our history—the new direction is the renewed appeal to educators to be "special" people with unique sensitivities and a spirit of growing up that puts them in touch with self and others, while saying *"I am responsible for the quality of my participation and leadership."*

Characteristics of Specific Interpersonal Techniques Used to Respond to Individual Differences

This section, focusing on the "how" to respond to individual differences, draws from techniques advanced by various theorists. For example, a teacher might decide to reinforce particular behavioral patterns, initiate discussion of the individual as resources, or restructure the classroom milieu, thereby reflecting approaches suggested by behaviorists, humanists, and psychoanalysts respectively.

In the interactional process involving all participants in the learning situation, various methods are used to focus on individual differences. A key factor in the interactional process is the constructiveness of the dialogue generated in assessing and evaluating the nature and significance of differences that prevail. Involved are the teacher-pupil and pupil-pupil dialogues—the interpersonal relationships—that develop as individuals in a group focus on what is to be done, the resources available and needed, and the outcomes that are to be anticipated. Experience has shown that such interpersonal relationships should be neither laissez-faire or unreasonably controlled. Systematic planning is essential if the task is to be completed in a manner that

---

[18] Warren G. Bennis, Edgar H. Schein, David E. Berlew, and Fred I. Steele, "Some Interpersonal Aspects of Self-Confirmation," in *Interpersonal Dynamics: Essays and Readings on Human Interaction,* ed. Warren G. Bennis (Homewood, Ill.: Dorsey Press, 1969), pp. 207-225.

respects the individual differences of each learner. More important, all participants—teacher as well as student—must remember that they enter into the learning experience with a unique repertoire of responses and knowledges that require assessment and evaluation.

Assessment of Differences

In deciding to respond to the uniqueness of the participants in the learning situation, the teacher is necessarily involved in assessment. The assessment process is a systematic activity that is both highly personal and interpersonal. As a personal activity it relies upon the knowledge, style, and aim (goal, attitude formation, lesson activity, competency or mastery of a content or skill) of the individual teacher initiating the process. As an interpersonal activity, it depends on data from informal dialogue with the student, peers, family, and others who know the student, as well as on the meaning the teacher gives to the formal profile of the student derived from objective testing.

The process includes looking at the classroom structure (and its resources) and the individuals involved (teacher and students), to determine what helping and holding forces facilitate or inhibit goal realization. Formal or informal testing devices facilitate information gathering. Formal devices may be the simple process of asking the students what they see as strengths or weaknesses and what are their areas of interest. Informal assessment can serve to initiate and develop dialogue with the student which can promote quality interaction. Formal assessment can show relationship of the individual to other members of the group along select dimensions. Both formal and informal testing serve to increase the teacher's knowledge of student differences. Assessment does not have an ordinal place in the system and should take place when it is decided that information is needed. Thus, a teacher may choose to assess a student trait at the beginning of her contact with him, at the completion of a task, or at any point during the interaction.

Planning Instruction

Assessment leads to designing of a specific network of learning activities—sometimes referred to as programming, blueprinting, contracting, or drafting. Designing the program aids both teacher and student in determining the sequence of activities and what material or personal resources are required. The process of designing the activities can be initiated by the teacher or the task of planning may be part of the learning activity of the student.

As the student "works through" the program design, certain choices are made : *what to do* (skill involved, instructional area); with *whom* (independently, small group, large group); *when* (immediately or at another scheduled or unscheduled time); *where* (in the classroom, corridor, library, or learning center); and *how* (scope and limitations of project). Having a program design expedites choices. The design should be subject to revision after consultation with the teacher and/or other participants involved in the project. Program designing can be done on an individual, small group, or whole class basis, depending on the task and its appropriateness for all or some of the class members. In the interactional process in which the program design is developed, the participants define each other's resources and experience the norms of the learning situation, as well as the physical resources in the classroom structure.

Conveying Respect for Individual Uniquenesses

The teacher who is a polished technician in feeling and projecting a valuing for individual uniqueness can through visual, vocal, and body language communicate that each member of the collective group is an individual. The reader has no doubt experienced the group leader who, when talking to a large group, was able to establish an intimacy similar to a dyad relationship. In communicating, a sense of regard and respect for individual differences should prevail as desires, interests, abilities, and goals are taken into account in deciding a group for individualized direction.

Projecting confidence in the students' ability will promote a seriousness as they participate in the learning process. Confidence is reflected in the time taken to discuss interest, attitude, and behavior. If in the interactional process the teacher spends the major portion of the time directing behavior among the students, self-directed activity and peer support are inhibited. Growth in the ability to direct self, and be aware of others should underly student and teacher goals in the learning situation. In an atmosphere in which participants exercise confidence and self-direction, a feeling of production rather than chaos should explain the "noise" in the work area.

Use of Group Projects

One way that teachers make provision for individual differences in classroom activities is the use of group projects. A "project," as used here, refers to any unit of work. It may vary in length from a few hours to several days or weeks. Even such a task as composing a paragraph can be thought of as a project. When assigned to individuals, the writing of a paragraph may become a dreary exercise for some; when undertaken by a group of students, it has the chance of becoming an alive and stimulating team creative effort. With several students participating, cross-stimulation can occur as they search for words for their "paragraph project" that will convey precise meanings and feelings. The fun of choosing words with the kind of care that an artist uses to select his colors and brushes can be infectious. Out of such a simple project, students can be guided to see that the paragraph is a viable form of presenting an idea to others—when it is well-ordered and polished to convey the meaning desired.

Group projects are useful in improving individual skills. Let us say that a teacher has recommended to three students that they need practice in writing. The three students team up in one corner of the room with the tools needed (e.g., paper, pencils, dictionary) to write a paragraph that both conveys meaning and is technically correct. To initiate the project a topic is selected by the students. One group member is chosen to "man the dictionary," another to write, and the third becomes an observer-evaluator for the effort. As they begin discussing which topic to write about, the teacher may intervene to make a suggestion or to test their interest, particularly if the discussion becomes nonproductive. The teacher's job is to maintain a bird's-eye view of the interaction—never to direct, yet to offer suggestions when needed and to help members of the group to assess the progress achieved. Because improvement of individual skills is a goal, the teacher will make certain that each gains understanding and practice on needed skill development.

As with all learning, evaluation is essential in group projects. Initial assessment occurs during the planning stage. Group members and the teacher will participate. As the project progresses, intermediate evaluations of progress will take place. Such evaluations usually take the form of a group conference with judgments being shared with the teacher. How long evaluation sessions will be or how formal they will become will depend on the nature and length of the project. The goal is to achieve a spirit of teamwork that focuses on the tasks to be completed. Assessments may relate to individual contributions as well as to the group attainment. They will move from one point of development to another, aiming to enhance student perceptions and to motivate continuing effort rather than to censure individuals or to turn the effort into an ordeal to be resisted.

When projects extend over several days or weeks, it is well to formulate a written design for the team effort. Such a long-term plan should provide goals for individuals as well as for the group as a whole. The teacher's job will be to make sure that the needs of all are considered when the project is planned. The group may need help in relating various individual needs to the total project. A teacher-student conference of a few minutes may be all that is required to initiate such a project. Additional progress conferences will help to keep it moving. The teacher who belabors a point, is too directive and concerned with the end product rather than with the total learning activity, may find it impossible to individualize 20-30 students. In contrast, the teacher who takes time to get the proper understanding between self and the student can help to initiate a project of this extent in a few days or weeks, depending upon the maturity, achievement, and ability of the student. This approach influences the knowledge and valuing of individual differences experienced by participants in the learning situation.

Time Schedule

The teacher should schedule adequate time for necessary guidance and conferences to initiate projects and evaluate ongoing and terminating projects. Below is an actual teacher's schedule. Please note that the teacher allows herself some "empty" time slots for work (i.e., record keeping, thinking, etc.). The schedule is posted for students to read so that they will operate within teacher availability.

The different time slots insure teacher mobility and involvement in students' projects. As an initiator, the teacher has orientated students to the understanding that they should plan time to see the teacher about new "project ideas." The teacher is available Monday morning and Tuesday, Wednesday, and Friday afternoons for such conferences. The student is orientated to sign up for a conference on the proper sheet, and it is the student's responsibility to remember his appointment.

	Monday	Tuesday	Wednesday	Thursday	Friday
9:10 – 10:00	Initiating Projects	Materials Inventory	Open	Evaluating Projects	Group Projects
10:00 – 11:00	Evaluating Projects	Progress Conferences	Conferences	Small Group Discussion	Progress Conferences
11:00 – 11:45	Open	Small Group Discussion	Planning	Open	Interest Projects
	Lunch	Lunch	Lunch	Lunch	Lunch
1:10 – 2:00	Conferences	Initiating Projects	Group Discussion	Progress Conferences	Interest Projects
2:10 – 2:50	Group Discussions	Open	Interest Projects	Small Group Discussion	Planning for Next Week
2:50 – 3:00	Group Planning	Group Planning	Group Planning	Group Planning	

When the teacher has a progress conference, she merely walks about the learning facility to see how the individual projects are coming. This can be, but need not be, a formal "sit down" conference. The evaluation conference usually takes on two forms. It can be more formal and consequential than the progress conference if the teacher chooses. The original or revised project goals (revised during the period of the "working through" of the project) are set up as criteria for determining excellence in the completion as well as working through of the project. Another evaluation conference can be a simple statement of agreement between the teacher and student that the student has completed his work on a project. The evaluation may have been made at each progress conference, thus necessitating no other comments.

Responding to individual differences does not necessarily involve one-to-one instruction or evaluation. The teacher's schedule can show several large- and small-group discussion time slots. The fruitfulness of group dynamics through group interaction is an essential part of the responding to individual differences and helps to keep the body of students working collectively as a community. If each individual is to have freedom to utilize the resources, he must respond to others and their needs as well as to his own desires. Group discussions on the common goals of the classroom community, the existing projects which are going on, and the added resources to the classroom keep the machinery of the program welded, oiled, and operating for all.

This group discussion time is also an excellent time to determine which students need help in particular skills and which are coming along as expected for ability, achievement, purpose, and total school goals per given grade or ability level.

The end-of-the-day group planning time is a time to regroup and settle before departing for home. The teacher may use the time to comment on the general atmosphere of the day, or individual students may wish to gripe or reflect on classroom activities. A brief discussion or teacher decision can determine if such an end-of-the-day session is profitable for a whole group, small group, or individual meeting.

Periodically, to let off steam, it is good to have a general gripe session. This gripe session can be another form of a conference simply for the point of giving the floor to a few students who are in need of expressing themselves. The teacher can also gripe, if unhappy about a classroom community problem.

The evaluation conference is for the opportunity of officially terminating a project; the progress conference for assessing productiveness; and the gripe conference for dealing with a problem before it becomes disruptive. There is also the counseling conference for dealing with an individual problem in the classroom community.

Any interaction can be called a conference if the desire is to reconstruct the situation and propose alternatives. This approach is encouraged because it demonstrates a model for improving the quality of interpersonal relations and personalizes the situation. Students also learn to see self in the situation and in the differences in conceptualizing, responding, and resolving.

Three final points should be emphasized in closing this section on interpersonal techniques. First, the specifics of responding to individual differences discussed here are flexible and valid, as they demand inclusion on their own merits in a given classroom. Second, it is necessary for the teacher to assess, design a course of action, and evaluate the productiveness of the new direction in a spirit that considers the differences of all participants in the learning situation. Finally, the different human variables of teacher and students influence the decision to initiate, maintain, and change the classroom process and structure. It is therefore expected that all individuals enter the situation with unique knowledge, values, and a repertoire of responses that can be influenced by the interactional process initiated and maintained by participants; and that individuals intermittently leave and reenter this situation as different individuals.

Promoting Sensitivity to Individual Differences

The position advanced in this chapter is that if more participants enter the learning situation having experienced a similar high valuing and knowledge of differences, it is likely that there would be a greater response to uniqueness. One could therefore expect the norm of continuous assessing, blueprinting, and evaluating of activities to be assumed with greater ease.

If, on the other hand, the participants enter the learning situation with limited experience in responding to differences, establishing the norms of continuous assessing, blueprinting, and evaluating would be helped by the teacher's efforts to sensitize participants to understand the reality and value of differences through a set of experiences. The method could involve providing case studies of events and situations and involving participants in the activity of analyzing the sequence, uniqueness, and relationship of events. In the process individuals are led to discover themselves as resources, and to create and define situations and their components. The method prepares the student for an interactional process that responds to differences—in which participants assess status of knowledge and self at a point in time; cultivate a direction through blueprinting, contrasting, and/or self and group negotiating; and reassess or evaluate knowledge and self at another point in time. In this interactional process, participants respond, adjust and change. The structure with its provision for minimal or great individualization facilitates responding through the traffic pattern and alternative it permits.

The teacher points the way in a manner that projects a shared goal of learning. The dynamic mix of differing participants becomes the resource which encourages cultivation of awareness and response mechanisms.

In responding to the reality of individual differences, freedom, confidence, and power are kept intact—while change and growth occur and are expected. We turn to Carl Rogers for a summation of the theory that supports the kind of instruction that is sensitive to individual differences: ". . . the degree to which I can create relationships which facilitate the growth of others as separate persons is a measure of the growth I have achieved in myself." [19]

[19] Carl Rogers, as quoted in the Preface of Milton Magenoff's *On Caring* (New York: Harper and Row, 1971).

7 A Systems Approach to the Theory for Teaching

**GUSTAVE J. RATH and
TOM McAULIFFE**

Systems and Systems Theory

A new perspective may be gained on problems and theories for teaching through systems concepts and systems analysis. The objective of a systems approach is to achieve a comprehensive view of a problem, with a systematic analysis of proposed solutions. What such an approach has to offer is a unifying framework for using and analyzing theories concerned with particular aspects of the process of teaching. This framework can aid both in solving particular problems—by helping to understand how theories can be applied to a problem—and in understanding and developing relationships between theories. After presenting a brief introduction to systems thinking and systems analysis, we will develop these applications more fully.

The first assumption of the systems approach is that there is some identifiable object (or collection of objects) which can be conceptually separated from its surroundings. The object is the *system* (classroom), and its surroundings are the *environment* (school). The distinction is always relative and to some extent arbitrary, and may be made in a different way for a different problem. For instance, one might ask, "Are the resource center and the classroom clearly separate?" In the present analysis, the environment is that which is relatively fixed and unchanging. It affects the system and is affected by it.

Usually some sort of interchange occurs between system and environment—materials, information, or energy may be passed between them. If the direction of interchange is from environment to system, the process is referred to as *input* to the system (e.g., a memo from the director of curriculum); if from system to environment, it is referred to as *output* from the system (report card).

Every system can be described in terms of entities comprising the system, attributes describing those entities, relationships between entities and attributes, and processes which change the state of the system. A more detailed view can be found in Miller and Rath (1971), Rath (1971), Churchman (1968), and Mesarovic et. al. (1970).

As an illustration of these ideas, consider a school system. Entities might include teachers, students, administrators, buildings, books, and supplies. Entities can in general be either permanent or temporary. In the present example, students, for instance, would be permanent if the time period under consideration were a year or less, but temporary if the period were several years. Attributes of a student might include age, grade, home address, and whether or not he is in school on a particular day. Relationships define the structure of the system. Susan is a student of Mr. Smith, and their class is in building X. Processes are changes in the state of the system. One hundred new students enter the school system; a student achieves new knowledge; a teacher becomes principal; or 75 students graduate.

There are two descriptive statements which capture much of the flavor of systems thinking. The first is that *one can never account for all properties of a system by simply describing the properties of its components*. The organization of the components must also be taken into account. This may seem obvious, but it is easy to forget or overlook. An example is the assertion that our bodies are worth only one or two dollars because that is the worth of the elements comprising it. This is like saying that a large computer is worth twenty dollars because it would bring that much as scrap metal. The computer is worth much more because of the way the metal is organized, and so are our bodies. The second statement describing systems thinking is *one can never change only one thing*. This can be considered a corollary of the first statement, and simply means that the elements of the universe are interconnected. Whenever one element is changed, those elements connected to it must change also.

A very important classification of systems is that of *open* versus *closed* systems. These two terms are opposite ends of a continuum describing the degree to which the systems structure can be modified. In a completely closed system, all possible contingencies have been accounted for in advance. Nothing is left to chance; users cannot affect system performance except in predetermined ways. A more open system, on the other hand, does not completely specify all alternatives. At some points, only a guideline is available to users, and they must decide what action to take.

Computer-assisted instruction systems provide an example that clarifies this distinction. A system typical of those currently being developed is similar in some ways to a programmed textbook. A specific topic is covered by presenting material and then asking specific questions. The response must match the correct answer exactly, except possibly in some trivial details. At any point, the response controls the sequence in which the material is presented. If an incorrect response

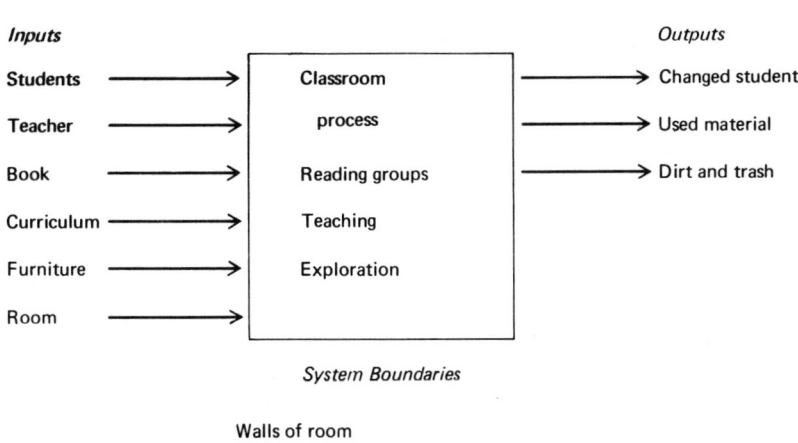

Figure 1

Segmenting a Problem Into Units

is given, some material may be repeated, or a more exhaustive set of exercises provided. If a correct response is given, the system goes on to the next problem or topic.

An alternative approach is to treat the computer as an information storage resource. The student can record any information he wants. He can then link together different information items, so that when he retrieves an item he is interested in, he is told of other related items. Thus if he is working on a term paper, he can use the system instead of keeping notes. He can also write simple programs—for example, to edit his information or to search for items containing certain words.

These two types of systems are not really competitive; they both have their place. The point is that in the second system the user can modify the information structure, while in the first system the user cannot modify the structure. The second is more open than the first.

The major application of systems theory in problem solving is in providing a check for consistency and completeness. What are the inputs? What are the outputs? What are the system boundaries? What subsystems are contained within the system and how are they interrelated? What processes transform the inputs into outputs? Application of these ideas can also assist in segmenting a complex problem into manageable units (see Figure 1).

Systems Analysis

Systems analysis is a formalized process of decision making, based on the assumption that all decisions are choices between alternative systems. Figure 2 illustrates the systems analysis paradigm.

The initial step is *problem formulation,* translating a vague feeling of need into a well-defined notion of what must be done. A well-formulated problem requires a way of knowing when it is solved and a possibility of solution. *Objectives* are then determined in view of the requirements of a decision-maker. Goals which must be reached before the problem can be considered solved are defined. *Criteria* are developed from the objectives which determine how the objectives will be met (these are precise, measurable representatives of the objectives).

In considering the problem, there are certain *resources* which can

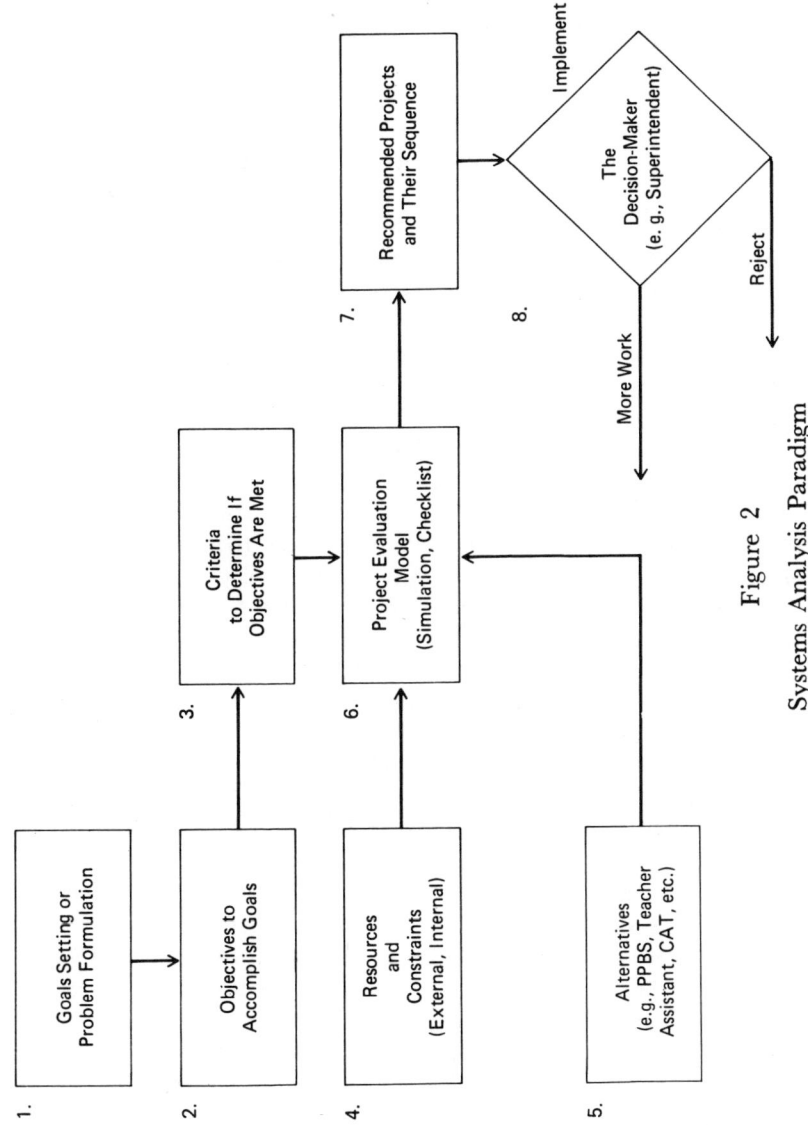

Figure 2
Systems Analysis Paradigm

be used and certain *constraints* which must be observed. Resources and constraints are one and the same : something is a resource if there is more than is required, and something is a constraint if there is not enough to meet the requirement. In attempting to solve the problem, a number of *alternatives* may be considered. Generating the alternatives may be the most difficult part of the process, and is the component requiring the greatest creativity.

After alternatives have been elaborated, there must be some way of deciding which one best meets the objectives while satisfying the resources and constraints. This is the function of the *evaluation procedure or model.* Some method must be worked out to choose between alternatives. This may range from simple checklists to elaborate schemes involving computer simulation or other complex measurement techniques.

A *scenario* is written for each alternative. This is a brief description of how it would be implemented, the effects it would have, its advantages and disadvantages—in general, a verbal description to give a feeling for the consequences of implementing that alternative. An important part of the scenario is the listing of key assumptions that have been made. The evaluations and scenarios are presented to the decision-maker, the individual who will make the final decision. This may be the same person who performs the analysis. There are two reasons for explicitly including the decision-maker in the process. First, inclusion emphasizes the time factor. The purpose of systems analysis is to assist in decision making, and need for a decision implies some limited time frame in which to work. Systems analysis thus differs from pure research—and that difference can have a profound effect on the process and the outcome. Not all factors can be considered; some potential alternatives may be overlooked, etc. Second, inclusion of the decision-maker emphasizes that systems analysis itself does not make the decision under consideration. It simply provides information, and it must be recognized that not all information relevant to the decision may be included. The actual decision is up to a person—a person who may have a vague, undefinable feeling that the recommended alternative is not really the best, or who may have private information not available to the systems analyst (such as information concerning a political debt).

We do not mean to suggest that the process sketched above should always be carried out in the same order. In one case, analysis may begin with sketching the alternatives, while in another, problem formulation may come first. All except the simplest problem will require a number of iterations of each step in the process. Objectives may be restated after evaluation methods are outlined; additional resources and constraints may be added when a new alternative is thought of.

Examples of Systems Analysis

To give a better feeling for the process of systems analysis, several examples of application to educational problems will be given.

EXAMPLE 1 : *Accommodating 500 new students in school district*

Consider first a hypothetical elementary school district with two school buildings. A subdivision of 500 houses is being built within the district, and there is an average of one school-age child in each house. The superintendent has to decide what to do with 500 new students.

Problem formulation : To integrate 500 new children into the school system.

Objectives : To maintain current class sizes and educational levels.
To minimize disruption during transitionary period.
To satisfy wishes of parents as much as possible.

Criteria : Standardized test scores.
Questionnaires filled out by teachers, students, and staff members.

Alternatives : To build new school.
To add wing to closest school.
To add wings to the two closest schools, shift boundaries.

Resources and constraints:	As boundaries are now, all new children fall within one of the school areas. Budgetary constraints exist but superintendent has power to request referendum to raise taxes. Parental attitudes and desires.
Evaluation:	Distribute questionnaires to residents explaining alternatives and asking preference. Base evaluation on weighted combination of questionnaire responses, ratings by administrators and building contractors of alternatives.

EXAMPLE 2: *Designing course in group dynamics*

Problem formulation:	How to set up assignments and assign grades in one-quarter undergraduate course in group dynamics.
Objectives:	To achieve some familiarity with current thought on group dynamics. To encourage independent thought and individuality, reliance on one's own analysis. To encourage examination of one's own and others' behavior in groups. To develop ability to analyze group processes.
Criteria:	Questionnaire filled out at beginning and end of quarter by students. Teacher observation of perceptiveness of students in classroom group situation. Student ratings of selves and each other.
Resources and constraints:	Ten weeks of class, meets 3 hours per week. Students have approximately 6 hours per week to devote to class. Students are freshmen and sophomores. Available books and journal articles. Library, classroom. Teacher's experience and training in group dynamics. Teacher's personality.

Alternatives: Reading.
Exams, quizzes.
Book reports.
Group or individual projects.
Papers.
Class participation.
Leading class on some topic.
Various combinations of some of the above.
Give students choices between alternatives or not.
Grading: done by teacher, by teacher and students together, or by students alone.

Evaluation: Informal consideration by teacher of merits of each alternative and combinations of alternatives.

EXAMPLE 3: *Decision by student in group dynamics class on how to organize his work*

Suppose the teacher in Example 2 ends up organizing the course as follows:

1. The teacher meets with each student individually at the beginning of the quarter to set up a study program.
2. There is a list of required readings and a list of suggested further readings.
3. Some combination of work is chosen from the following:
   a. Short paper that includes brief survey of literature.
   b. Field study and write-up—observation of some group at work.
   c. Project with one or more other students.
   d. Leading class for part of one class period.
   e. Long paper on some topic of interest.
4. Teacher and student jointly decide on grade at end of quarter.

The problem for the student, then, is to decide what combination of work he should choose from (2) and (3) above.

His objectives:	To learn about himself and how he can better relate to others. To find out what group dynamics is about. To take more initiative in groups. To get an A in the course because he wants to go to graduate school.
His resources and constraints:	Number of hours he can spend on course. His abilities: good at reading and analytical papers. Teacher's concept of amount of work required for an A.

Even if the student were to go through this procedure, he doubtless would not bother with developing criteria or a formalized evaluation procedure. The example is intended to show that the systems analysis paradigm can be a useful tool in clarifying any decision—even informal ones—in which some of the steps may be performed without explicit consideration. It is simply an aid to clear thinking.

Scientific Theory and Systems Analysis

The preceding description of systems analysis presents a straightforward view, one that would provoke little disagreement among practicing systems analysts. It leaves a great deal unsaid, however, about the relationship of systems analysis to other intellectual and creative endeavors, and about the psychology of systems analysis. This section explores these two areas, with the aim of providing a deeper understanding of systems analysis and how it can be used to promote thoughtful and constructive change in schools or in any other system.

First, then, how does the systems analysis process relate to other intellectual disciplines? Systems analysis is primarily a *knowledge process*: like science, it is a method for investigating a particular corner of reality and (hopefully) coming up with a useful description.

This classification of systems analysis in the same category as science goes against a traditional intellectual dichotomy. Systems analysis is a design technique, and as such can be categorized with such professions as engineering, law, and architecture. A strict separation has long been maintained between pure science, a *descriptive* process; and systems analysis, a *prescriptive* process. The following passage from Herbert Simon gives one characterization of this dichotomy.

> . . . Certain phenomena are "artificial" in a very specific sense: They are as they are only because of a system's being molded, by goals or purposes, to the environment in which it lives. If natural phenomena have an air of "necessity" about them in their subservience to natural law, artificial phenomena have an air of "contingency" in their malleability by environment.
>
> The contingency of artificial phenomena has always created doubts as to whether they fall properly within the compass of science . . .
> . . . I thought I began to see in the problem of artificiality an explanation of the difficulty that has been experienced in filling engineering and other professions with empirical and theoretical substance distinct from the substance of their supporting sciences. Engineering, medicine, business, architecture and painting (and, we might add, teaching) are concerned not with the necessary but with the contingent—not with how things are but with how they might be—in short, with design.[1]

It is not our intention to lessen the importance of this distinction. It is rather to suggest that the validity of the distinction has perhaps blinded us to other areas in which science and the design professions are much more similar than we usually realize. The reason for pointing out these similarities is double-edged: they tell us something both about scientific theory and about systems analysis and other design professions, including teaching.

We will discuss three specific similarities between science and systems analysis. These are not exhaustive, but they give a good picture of the areas held in common. The first similarity is between *theories* and *models*. It should be clearly pointed out, however, that a distinction is usually made between the conceptual frameworks used by science (theories) and by systems analysis (models). A model is often regarded as a heuristic guide; it is useful for solving a particular

---

[1] Herbert A. Simon, *The Sciences of the Artificial* (Cambridge: MIT Press, 1969), pp. ix–xi.

problem or for looking at a problem in a certain way, but we do not necessarily believe that it is an accurate representation of reality. For example, hydraulic models are often used to teach about electricity : water flowing through pipes is analogous to electricity flowing through wire; water pressure is analogous to voltage, and so on.

A theory, on the other hand, is something in which we can believe. It is intended to capture the truth about some aspect of reality. Admitting that a theory can never be the complete truth, it is nevertheless our best approximation to reality. For example, the theory of electricity holds that the flow of electricity is actually movement of electrons, components of matter having a negative charge. The flow is the result of attractive and repulsive forces of electrons and protons. Even though no one has directly observed electrons, they are believed to exist. We *believe* our theories.

We assert that this distinction between models and theories is a misleading one. It is misleading because it might tend to give more plausibility to theories than they deserve, and less plausibility to models than they deserve. Models are just as truthful as theories in the areas in which they are intended to be used. Nevertheless the objection could be raised that even if this is true, it is sometimes difficult—and perhaps impossible—to see limits to their applicability. Models might therefore lead to mistaken ideas and inferences. Continuing the electricity example, if we cut a pipe in a hydraulic system, water will pour out onto the floor. If we cut a wire in an electrical system, however, electrons do not pour out onto the floor—they simply stop flowing. Had we blindly followed our model, we would have been led to false conclusions.

To counter this argument for dissimilarity, however, it need only be noted that the same argument applies to theories; in a specific situation, it is often difficult to decide whether a particular theory is relevant or not. For example, reinforcement theory holds that a given behavior can be made to occur more frequently by providing an appropriate reinforcement whenever the target behavior occurs. This principle seems to apply, for instance, to verbal behavior. As Rogers reports : "Verplanck, Greenspoon, and others have shown that operant conditioning of verbal behavior is possible in a relationship. Very briefly, if the experimenter says 'Mmm,' or 'Good,' or nods his head after certain types of words or statements, those classes of words tend to increase because of being reinforced. It has been shown that by using such procedures one can bring about increases in such diverse verbal categories as plural nouns, hostile words, statements of opinion." [2]

A logical extension of this idea is to think that any aspect of verbal behavior can be modified, given the appropriate reinforcer. A body of evidence is developing, however, that indicates that humans come equipped with some innate capacity for language production (see Slobin, 1971). All languages seem to share some structural features, and linguistic developmental processes of all children seem to have some sequence in common. Operant conditioning techniques would probably be ineffective therefore in attempting to modify aspects of verbal behavior related to word sequences or grammatical structure. At some point, then, reinforcement theory no longer applies, but it is unclear where that point is. Theories thus contain the same weakness as models: their range of application is never completely specified. This shortcoming is of great importance and will be dealt with at greater length in the following section, "The Knowledge Process."

Another feature shared by theories and models is that they are both schematic representations of the piece of reality with which they are intended to deal. In both cases there are certain observed data which are used to organize or provide a framework for the theory or model. There are always some data, however, which do not fit the framework. The point is that a theory is not *identical* with reality any more than a model is. It is an abstract representation of some aspects of reality which are considered more important than others.

The second similarity between science and systems analysis (and other design activities) is closely related to the first: theory building and model building are both *active,* constructive processes. Science is often regarded as an essentially passive processs, as contrasted with the active process of model building: a body of data is examined and regularities found; scientific laws are statements of these regularities; scientific theories are collections of laws. This view is misleading for

---

[2] Carl R. Rogers, *On Becoming a Person* (Boston: Houghton Mifflin, 1961), p. 45.

two reasons. First, the process of data collection is not a passive activity. Implicit in any observation process are assumptions about what is worth observing and what is not. There is always an active selection of data. Moreover, once a body of data has been collected, the process of organizing it is an active effort to build a framework which fits as closely as possible. Thus scientific progress is not the even, cumulative process that it is often portrayed as. It is not achieved simply by the addition of one isolated fact or law after another. Components of a theory have complex interrelationships, and to some extent a theory stands or falls as a whole.[3] A theory attempts to be a coherent system of concepts, and modification of one component often requires modification of others also. With this perspective, the kinship of theory building with model building and other systems analysis activities can be clearly seen.

The third point of similarity between science and systems analysis —that science and systems analysis are both highly personal enterprises —is more an effort to remove a false distinction than to build bridges. Because of its methods, science often seems incomprehensible and distant from other means of knowing. Of paramount importance in science, for instance, is the principle of *reproducibility of results.* Science is a collective enterprise, and the claims of one scientist are not sufficient to gain widespread acceptance of a new result; other scientists must be able to reproduce the same results. This need for replication produces a corresponding need for rigorous specification of the experimental situation and of the expected results. This need in turn produces complex methodology and tools of measurement and comparison, such as statistical methods of description and tests of significance. To an observer of science, these methodological complexities take on much more importance than the conceptual content.

Contrast this situation with that of teachers. As much as any scientist, they are concerned with obtaining reliable information about the children in their classes. Often, however, they do not have to justify the reliability of that knowledge to anyone except themselves

---

[3] For a comprehensive treatment of this topic, see T. S. Kuhn, *The Structure of Scientific Revolutions,* 2nd ed. (Chicago: University of Chicago Press, 1970).

and need not specify the sources of knowledge. Their methods of knowing can thus be much more informal than those of science, and the knowledge seems to be of a more personal nature when compared with the collective knowledge of science.

The collective aspect of science is just one part of the scientific process, however; and viewing it in isolation tends to exaggerate the gap between science and less formal methods of knowing. Personal knowledge and informal processes are of great importance to science at two points in the total process. First, hypotheses which are tested using rigorous methods can be generated by informal observation, intuition, hunches, guesses, and wild ideas and associations. The scientific method can be visualized as a process of exploration, hypothesis generation, and hypothesis selection or testing. The rigor of science is found in the testing process, and not in the generation process. Generation of new ideas is thus as informal and personal a process in science as anywhere else. Second, widespread acceptance of an idea depends on its adoption by individual scientists. Each one of them must accept it as a personal belief. Many factors other than experimental evidence may enter into a decision to accept or reject a hypothesis or theory, such as compatibility with existing beliefs or value system.

To summarize this third point of similarity, when the scientific process is viewed in its entirety as a human enterprise, its technical aspects are seen in proper perspective, subordinate to the process of personal knowing. Scientific methodology merely sharpens our perceptions.[4]

The Knowledge Process

The similarities between science and systems analysis extend beyond the static points of comparison examined in the previous section. The psychological processes of scientific investigation and systems analysis have many features in common. Indeed, the conten-

---

[4] The view of science as a highly personal enterprise is discussed by Michael Polanyi, *Personal Knowledge* (Chicago: University of Chicago Press, 1958).

tion of this section is that all processes of concept formation and conceptual change (of which science and systems analysis are subcategories) share basic frameworks. There exist three basic dimensions for describing all these methodologies: *exploratory (a priori); normative empirical; and study-experiment* (Thompson and Rath, in press).

The following analysis of concept formation and conceptual change should be of interest to teachers because, as much as any profession, the teaching activity relies on this process to generate valid information about the classroom and students in it.

A certain openness to change or to new ideas must be cultivated. Concepts form an interlocking network, and change often involves shifts and adjustments of concepts only peripherally related to the focus of change. An analogy might help clarify the point. Suppose a principal of a school decides that the functions one of his teachers performs should be changed. Unless the change is ot a very limited sort, he will also have to consider changing the assignments of the other members of his staff. The persons affected are those that the focal person interacts with in performing his job, such as other teachers on the same team or teachers in the same grade. Thus, a change conceived of as involving a single person might turn out to involve a number of others. The degree of change which the principal can effect is largely determined by the extent to which he can restructure not just individual jobs, but also relationships between all concerned.

Similarly, to be able to change concepts, there must be a certain openness—a willingness to question not just isolated concepts, but whole networks of concepts. This need for openness is captured in a model of personal change developed by Warren Bennis and others (1969), based on ideas of Kurt Lewin. According to the model, the complete change process has three parts: a period of unfreezing, when the motivation to change is created; a period of changing, when development of new assumptions, beliefs, and ideas occurs; and a period of refreezing, when the changes are integrated with other beliefs, and adjustments are made in relationships. There is recognition in this schema that our concepts and beliefs form networks of mutual support, and that it is difficult to disconfirm a single belief unless others are called into question also. Thus, the period of unfreezing is necessary, during which an openness to change is developed.

Openness, of course, is always a question of degree. There are some beliefs which are tentative and easy to give up, and there are others that may never be open to question, or even to awareness. We might think of a continuum of openness, with one end labeled open, tentative, explicit, easy to change, aware, and the other end labeled closed, certain, implicit, hard to change, unaware. The more a person can remain on the open end of the continuum, the more extensive the changes of which he is capable.

There are two other topics that are related to openness, and a brief discussion of them should add more substance to the conceptual framework we have been discussing. The first is *empathy*. Carl Rogers defines empathic understanding in the form of questions.

> . . . Can I let myself enter fully into the world of his feelings and personal meanings and see these as he does? Can I step into his private world so completely that I lose all desire to evaluate or judge it? Can I enter it so sensitively that I can move about in it freely, without trampling on meanings which are precious to him? Can I sense it so accurately that I can catch not only the meanings of his experience which are obvious to him, but those meanings which are only implicit, which he sees only dimly or as confusion?[5]

The relationship of empathy to openness is clear if empathy is seen as the ability to temporarily rearrange one's conceptual network to agree more closely with someone else's. Such rearrangement is possible only if one is open. Empathy, then, is an important ability for obtaining valid knowledge about others, not distorted by translation which fails to do justice.

The second related topic is *observation*. When someone is learning about a new situation, he is effective to the extent that he can observe minute details without prejudging, to the extent that he is open to new experience. Karen Horney describes this ability well in writing about the task of the psychoanalyst.

> The analyst's interest does not focus upon one part of the patient, not even upon the disturbed part, but necessarily embraces the whole personality. Since he wants to understand its entire structure, and since he does not know offhand what may be more relevant and what less, his attention must absorb as many factors as possible.

[5] Rogers, *op. cit.*, p. 53.

> ... The analyst's specific observations, however, are an indispensable part of the analytic process. They constitute a systematic study of unconscious forces as revealed in the patient's free associations. To these the analyst listens attentively, trying not to select any one element prematurely but to pay an even interest to every detail.[6]

Openness, and the related abilities of empathy and observation, are thus crucial components of any process of knowing. They are crucial even in those areas, such as science or systems analysis, where they are thought of (when they are thought of at all) as secondary to technical expertise. They have been presented here as prerequisites to conceptual change, but they are also integral components of the change process itself. Change of any complexity will involve a number of cycles before a satisfactory state is achieved, and openness is needed throughout the process to prevent premature termination. That change process and its cycles are the next topics of discussion.

The description of conceptual change given here is based partly on an important assumption. One is never aware of everything that might be relevant to a given problem, so observation is guided by a framework. That is, some data are considered potentially important, while others are ignored or not even considered; these choices represent a set of assumptions about the problem.

On the other hand, any framework is going to be inaccurate or irrelevant in some aspects because it is based on incomplete data. The data are incomplete because one of the purposes of the framework is to guide further data collection. It should be clear, then, that conceptual change is neither a slow fitting of data into a preconceived framework, nor a steady, cumulative development of a model from raw data. In fact, we seem to have created a paradox, in which we cannot collect data without some sort of framework, and we cannot build a useful framework without first collecting data.

How do we escape from the paradox we have constructed? The first step is to realize that it accurately represents some aspects of the process of problem solving or conceptual change: a good problem-solver will collect data that turn out to be useless, and he will

---

[6] Karen Horney, *Self-Analysis* (New York: W. W. Norton, 1968), pp. 125–126.

formulate hypotheses and tentative solutions that turn out to be incorrect. The trick is to make relatively small mistakes throughout the process, and not wait until the end and discover that the entire product is worthlesss. An analogy can be made with a ship captain. On a long voyage, he is not always heading in the proper direction, and he frequently makes midcourse corrections. He does not blindly sail until he comes to land, only to find out that he should have been going in the opposite direction.

The process of conceptual change has a two-part cycle (although in reality the two parts cannot be separated as neatly as they are here). First, a tentative model is constructed which guides the data-collection process. Second, the data collected is used to evaluate and modify the model. This cycle is repeated until the solution reached is deemed satisfactory. Each time, some of the data collected during the previous cycle may be discarded, and some parts of the model may be modified. The end product might bear little or no resemblance to the original conception. Another way of looking at this is to say that any attack on a problem with our intellectual tools is double-edged : we will learn something about the problem, but (if we are open) we will also learn something about our tools.

A person can thus pull himself up by his bootstraps : his initial model may be bad, but it contains enough accurate assumptions that some of the collected data are useful. They suggest some changes in the model. The updated model is an improvement, so the data collected the second time through are more relevant, and so on.

Finally, once a model has been assembled, there are still decisions that must be made concerning its application in various situations. It must always be remembered that models are subordinate to the desires, feelings, and thoughts of their users. They must be regarded as tools that can be amended when they cease to correspond with our wishes. They cannot make all decisions that fall within their realm. Models are also shaped by our values. For example, they reflect decisions about what is worth studying. At times it may be necessary not just to make additions or slight modifications, but to modify the basic structure.

Given that a model has been adopted, vigilance must still be maintained against self-deception when attempting to apply it in a specific situation. Any such model is only a crude approximation to the segment of reality with which it is intended to deal. Discretion is always required, therefore, in applying it to solving a particular problem. Knowledge, insight, and feelings not contained in the model must be used to determine whether the fit between model and reality is close enough to have confidence in the conclusions.

Our models can never include all of our knowledge; we cannot put everything we know into the form of explicit rules. We must always reserve the right to disbelieve our inventions and to place our faith in practiced intuition.

By way of summary of the last two sections, it might be worthwhile to present our conception of the ideal systems analyst. Technical expertise might be important in some circumstances, but it is secondary to the psychological characteristics described here; he need not be good at technical details, in other words. Instead, he is aware that system characteristics are determined more by system organization, relationships, and networks of entities than by qualities of individual entities. He is not bounded by verbal definitions, initial problem statements, stereotypes, conventional classifications, or other static representations of the flowing world. He is open to experience, in the sense in which we discussed it earlier. He is empathic in his relationships with others, skillful at seeing things from their point of view. He is a good observer of details; he is able to absorb the *Gestalt* of the environment, to shape conceptual categories to fit what he has seen. He does not force observations into preconceived boxes.

Relationship of Other Chapters to the Systems Analysis Framework

It should be evident from what has been written that we consider the *process* of problem solving to be as important as any specific *content* or problem solutions that are achieved. The reason for this has to do with the complexity of the problems being tackled. A classroom, for instance, is impossible to understand completely. A solution to any problem, therefore, is necessarily only partially correct, or applicable only under certain conditions. To function effectively in such an environment, then, a teacher must not only understand existing solutions, but she must understand how to apply them, and how to modify them or come up with her own new solutions.

In the spirit of this orientation toward the process of problem solving or conceptual change, we intend to quickly examine the other chapters in this volume to give an insight into the tools they add to the problem-solving process. We will do this by relating them to the framework we constructed in the previous two sections. This examination will not be exhaustive; many other aspects of the chapters could be examined in the same light. Chapter 1, "Scientific Theory for Teaching: Its Nature and Role" (Park, Stone and Barron), is concerned with largely the same area that we are. According to the authors, "The hypothetico-deductive model of explanation purports to be a model of all causal explanation (pp. 14–15)," and we would want to say the same about our model of conceptual change. The two approaches are looking at two sides of the same coin, or at the outside and inside of the same phenomenon. They are discussing the logical structure and external form of causal explanation, and we are discussing the process by which causal explanations are arrived at.

The section in Chapter 1 titled "The Role of Theory in Practice" and our discussion of the limits of applicability of conceptual systems together form a comprehensive set of warnings about the limitations of theories or models. We are cautioning that the fit of a model to a specific situation is always a question of judgment by the user; it is essentially a technical problem. Park, Stone, and Barron are cautioning that even if the model does fit the situation accurately, care must be taken not to reach unjustified conclusions stated in the form of *oughts*. We feel that understanding a model may lead one to new insights (which require further testing), even though it is quite inaccurate.

In Chapter 2, "From Theories for Learning to Theories for Teaching," Mathis and McGaghie say, "... the architecture of a theory for teaching must be comprehensive and harmonious (p. 34)." They show concern about the lack of an integrative psychological framework on which to base such a theory for teaching. We would also urge development of an integrative framework and harmonious theory for reasons similar to theirs. During the evolution of any theory, numerous additions and modifications will occur. Because of the interrelatedness of components of a theory, changing any one of them will inevitably affect others. Unless these other components are changed also, internal contradictions and discrepancies will arise; thus, a process of *mutual adjustment* of concepts must occur. Drawing ideas indiscriminately from separate theories circumvents the mutual adjustment provided by an integrative framework. Validated combinations which are drawn for specific purposes may be pragmatically useful in the interim.

There are two connections which we would like to make between Petrie's Chapter 3, "The Believing in Seeing," and our chapter. The first is related to our statement that all data collection is active, in the sense that it is guided by some framework that determines which data are important and which are not. Petrie's chapter serves to point out that the framework need not be an explicit model or set of assumptions, but can be the very structure of the perceptual mechanism. For example, he says:

... In a hierarchy of perceptions there is no ground-floor level of perceptions. *All* perception is conceptually loaded (p. 58).

... In short, observational categories are theory-dependent and there is no basic predeterminable set of observational categories to which we can refer (p. 65).

The second connection between the two chapters has to do with the application of a theory or model to a particular situation. As we pointed out, "Our models can never include all of our knowledge; we cannot put everything we know into the form of explicit rules" (p. 158). Petrie shows that at least some of that additional, implicit knowledge is contained in the organization of our perceptions.

... There is, in principle, no way in which a mechanical recipe can be given [to the student] to apply the theory to the problems. Rather, his perceptual experience must come to him organized under the categories of the theory he has learned (p. 53).

... perceptual experience must come to be organized in accordance with the theory before it can be applied (p. 55).

... recipes "work" only if one perceives the appropriate situations in which to use them (p. 59).

Systems analysis is not a recipe, it gives a basis on which to apply perception. Systems analysis may serve as a method to attempt the achievement of successful organization.

The perspective of Chapter 4, "Systems Conflict in the Learning Alliance" (Bohannan, Powers, and Schoepfle), corresponds closely with ours. In general, the authors are concerned as we are with the process of problem solving, or conflict reduction. In particular, many of their ideas are closely related to our concept of openness. They stress the need for self-awareness, and the kinship between our chapters is made more apparent by pointing out the relationship between openness and self-awareness. Self-awareness is, in fact, a prerequisite for openness as we have discussed it. Openness, in turn, allows for change. As Bohannan, Powers, and Schoepfle say, "There is a direct and inescapable relationship between the teacher's self-knowledge and the teacher's ability to avoid creating conflict in the classroom. Unexamined goals are unchangeable goals" (p. 93).

The second relationship we wish to discuss between the two chapters centers on the point made in Chapter 4 that in psychotherapy and ethnography, the entire self is used as an instrument. We would urge that this point of view is equally important to all professions whose concerns are related to human behavior. It is highly compatible with our beliefs. For example, consider Bohannan, Powers, and Schoepfle's description of the task of the ethnographer: "Learning in an ethnographic situation is not like learning to be a scientist, where there is a body of knowledge to be mastered. The ethnographer must learn, rather, whatever it is that these people want to teach her. What they *want* to teach her is the most significant part of her data." (p. 83).

Compare this with what we said earlier in this chapter: "[The systems analyst] . . . is not bounded by conventional classifications . . . he is open to experience . . . he is empathic in his relationship with others, skillful at seeing things from their point of view . . . He is able to . . . shape conceptual categories to fit what he has seen. He does not force observations into preconceived boxes" (p. 158).

There is tension between the desire to make our theories all-inclusive and detailed, and the reality that individual decisions must inevitably be made largely on the basis of personal and social values. Our theories may guide us, but no matter how comprehensive they become, the gap will always exist. Chapter 5, "Assessing Alternative Teaching-Learning Alliances" (Epperson), argues that we need not for that reason throw up our hands and choose wildly. Epperson places theory in its proper complex context of functioning human beings, working with different perspectives, and provides a basis for systematizing our value choices. Both his chapter and ours express an appreciation of the complexities of reality, and of the need for an ecological approach to theory or models—studying and building them in their natural habitats, facing up to the difficult problems involved in their application.

Individualization, as discussed by Cross and Fields in Chapter 6, "Influence of Individual Differences on Instructional Theories," is a recognition of the complexity of the classroom, and of the fact that complexity need not be overwhelming, but instead can be made to work to promote learning. This brings up an important point, the inherent relationship between three concepts: complexity, openness of a system, and relative importance of process as opposed to content.

The more *complex* the system, the more difficult it becomes to determine the best solution to a problem in the system, or to anticipate the best way of achieving a specific goal. It thus becomes more and more important to design an *open* system, one that can modify its structure, when necessary, to best attack a specific problem. In such a system, more and more design or control effort will go into the ongoing *process* at the expense of specific goals or problem solution. This change in emphasis is illustrated by two quotations from Cross and Fields:

> ... The teacher's job is to maintain a bird's-eye view of the interaction—never to direct, yet to offer suggestions when needed and to help members of the group to assess the programs achieved (p. 133).
>
> ... The teacher who belabors a point, is too directive and concerned with the end product rather than with the total learning activity, may find it impossible to individualise 20–30 students (p. 134).

Individualization is a means, or process, rather than an end. The process is adapted to the specific makeup of the class, including teacher's characteristics:

> ... the individual teacher asks of self *not* "Do I possess the 'proper' psychological and pedagogical virtues?" but rather "What kind of person am I and how may I make the most of my uniqueness in helping children to learn?" (p. 129).

Thus there is no fitting of activities to preconceived categories, but evolution of structure from unique qualities of participants. The systems analysis process is available to the teacher so that solutions to problems arising from these unique qualities may be achieved. It may be applied to the teacher, to the student or to the learning activity.

Use of Theory in Systems Analysis

The systems analysis paradigm, as described in Figure 2, uses theory in several ways. The theory may be used to formulate the problem. A well-formulated problem requires that there is some hope of the solution. The theory may be the basis for that hope. Einstein, for instance, established theoretically that $E = MC^2$. That established the possibility of the conversion of matter into energy, which then became the basis of the atomic bomb and the nuclear power industry. The theory was necessary to formulate the problem of how to build these devices. A well-formulated problem has some way of telling whether one has achieved a solution. A good theory tells you what information to collect to support or reject the theory. Theory thus serves as a key cornerstone of the problem-formulation process. Putting it another way, a theory suggests what a decision-maker may want, as well as what an organization needs, and therefore becomes the basis for establishing the objectives of the theory.

The acceptance of the Freudian theory, for example, establishes a model which states that many people are sick, but can be cured with a prescribed method. Therefore, one may formulate the objective of curing people through psychotherapy. The decision-maker who believes in psychotherapy may then support proposals of studies to determine how psychotherapy may be best used. Today, behavior modification might fit this role. Decision-makers who believe in a different theory may prefer it. So the objective of many studies may be based on how to do behavioral modification better. Thus the theory which establishes objectives also serves to generate the criteria to be used.

Theories are also an important part of evaluating alternatives. Theory helps to determine a structure of objectives, criteria, and resources and constraints so that alternatives can be evaluated. Theory indicates what conditions should be studied. For example, in a study to evaluate several types of automated instructional equipment, a theory will suggest what are the important factors. An economic systems theory would indicate that such things as maintainability, operability, cost/effectiveness are important. A humanistic theory would suggest that one should consider the response of the student to these devices and see how it helps him develop his potential, etc.

Use of Systems Analysis on Theories

The systems analysis model can be used to evaluate alternative theories. Let's say that the objective is to develop a management philosophy for a school. This will be operationalized by stating that the management philosophy will be one which will increase the scores on children's behavioral standardized tests, such as the Iowa test, and increase their positive attitudes toward schools as measured through a special instrument developed for the school system.

Three competitive theories could be an operant conditioning view of education, a psychodynamic approach, and a progressive-education approach. Resources and constraints would include such items as "Does one understand the theory?" and "How many in the system can use it?" A system with many trained psychologists and psychiatrists may profit much more from a psychodynamic view than a system without such resources. A set of criteria designed to meet an objective could be developed for theories. This set might include the applicability to grades from K through 8, the ability to apply across subject matters, or the amount of time necessary to implement the recommended changes from the theory. On some basis, weights will have to be assigned to these different theories and one can then decide which theory best carries out the job. The systems analysis paradigm therefore could be a useful way to help choose and decide what theories may be used within a system. Theory concatenation is an important concept which will be discussed next.

Theory may emphasize several viewpoints. It may be used to describe the state of the student (e.g., psychodynamic view, developmental view like Erikson's, or learning psychological view like Guthrie's). On the other hand, other theories support process views. A Skinnerian view of the world, for instance, concentrates on the process of changing behavior. It does not define in great lengths what is current behavior or what future behavior should be. It very clearly establishes an efficient methodology of achieving whatever goals are set. A humanistic approach like Maslow's level-of-actualization approach does not really present a *way* of reaching different levels. Moreover, it very strongly suggests that some levels are better than others. The problem is that many of these theories cover different parts of the process. It turns out that a psychodynamic viewpoint may establish man's problems and where man should be, while behavioral approaches may strongly suggest how to take him from one to the other. Such a synthesis is what we are trying to foster.

Theories can be concatentated, thus bringing together elements from several theories; and applying these several elements correctly is a very important step, as it allows one to synthesize the theories. System analysis technology may be helpful in doing this; in particular, flow charts and structural diagrams may help in synthesizing the theories (see Chapter 5).

Requirements and Specifications of the Theory for Teaching

We think about teaching as involving students, teaching systems, and an external environment, as shown in Figure 3.

A theory for teaching must be able to describe the current state of the entities involved. What is the state of a student? What does he know? What does he desire to know? What is his physical condition? What is his mental state? What is his motivation? What are the forces acting upon him?

When describing a teacher one must consider his or her goals, motivations, techniques, experiences, feeling about students, feelings about media, and feelings about the school system. There may also exist physical devices, media, books, audiovisual equipment, classrooms, library, and other devices and systems which are available and

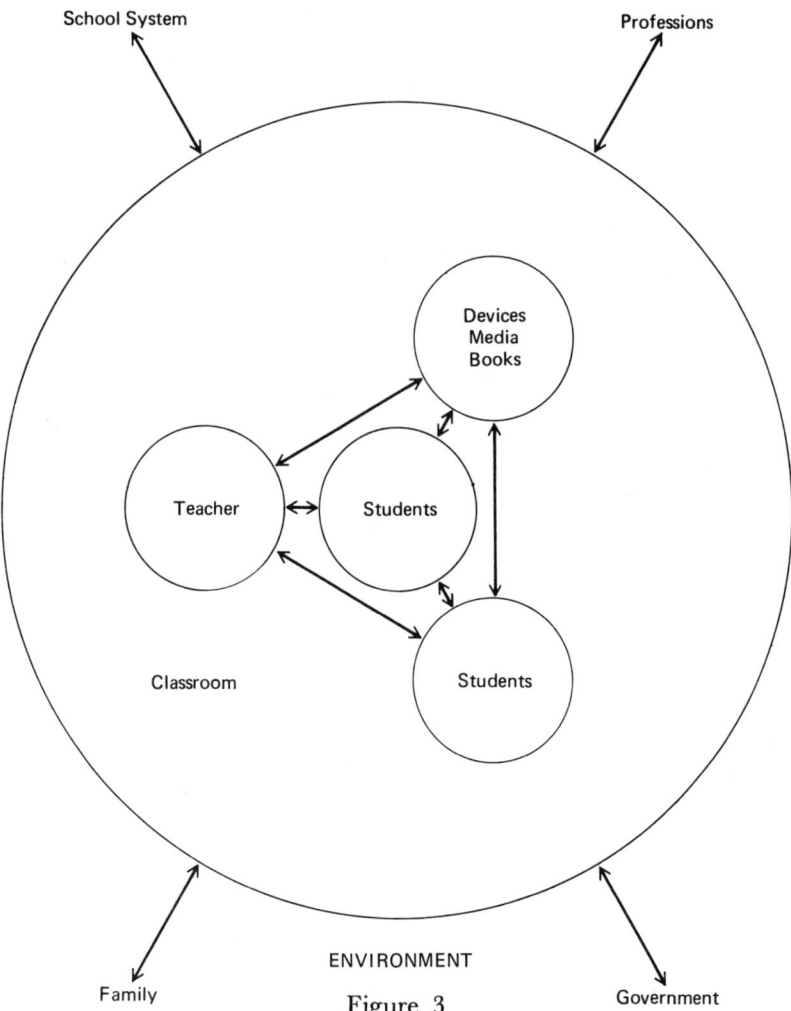

Figure 3
Entities That a Theory for Teaching Must Account for

involved in the teaching process. Other characteristics to be accounted for are the capacity, the flexibility, and the cost of the system. Lastly, there is an environment which impinges upon all of these—which includes the family, the school system, society, professions, the city, and all of the other environments which have demands upon and will ultimately accept the student. There also must exist ways of determining what is desired by these external influences and what are the values ascribed to the current conditions. For example, is the knowledge of Latin good or bad for the students?

The prediction of the future states of the student and the teacher is important. The prediction of the future states involves (1) knowing the current state and (2) determining the desired state and being able to predict how changes of a given type will alter things. Will there be changes in the student, the faculty, the devices, or the environment which will make it possible?

A theory for teaching should be able to predict future states. For example, a future state may involve going to individualized nongraded classrooms, using computer-assisted instruction, or relaxing the level at which students must maintain a cumulative average.

The effects of external forces on the system must be predictable; for example, the effects on student-teachers and educational media of the family demands of babysitting; the community's desire to have a library or a museum; the impact of the political ambitions or desires of the members of the community on the educational system. The allocation of money and resources to schools as opposed to other competing systems must also be understood in terms of its impact on teaching.

The ease or probability that certain states can be accomplished must be predictable. How does one motivate teachers and students to change? How can one control the rate and the amount of change from current states to future states? A theory must yield the systems and formulas for understanding the above changes.

A theory must also cover special cases of interest which deal with the number of entities involved. These include one-to-one, one-to-many, many-to-one, and many-to-many, as well as those cases in which the student is interacting with media through mechanical processes. We will consider each one of these separately.

A theory for teaching should be able to handle the one-to-one relationships, which include teaching, tutoring, and counseling. One-to-one formats include the interactions between a graduate student and his research supervisor, giving a student remedial help, and keeping a grade school student after class by a teacher. One-to-one arrangements are very process oriented because of the high degree of feedback between the student and the teacher. This feedback must be understood and explained. The motivation aspect of one-to-one is also important to comprehend. Many feel that one-to-one is the best type of teaching possible. It may be so, but it is not usually the most cost-effective.

One-to-many is a very traditional model. The most common example is the lecture. Another example is the laboratory with each person doing an experiment while the professor wanders about. The art professor with a class of painting students, in which he goes around commenting on each individual's creative work, is another mode. In some cases, the teacher's job may be distribution and presentation of knowledge; in other cases, it may be strictly a question of giving feedback, advice, or evaluation. This is often not satisfactory to many students because they do not get as much attention as in a one-to-one relationship, but it is much more cost-effective. If the attention is not needed or is counterproductive, a student should get less attention.

The many-to-one situation is not very common. It occurs, for instance, during doctoral and qualifying examinations when several faculty members may question and educate one student. It may also happen in research, where one student is working with a group of researchers as a team. Obviously, from a cost-effectiveness and efficiency viewpoint this is very inefficient, but with the use of several people in these special situations it is quite possible to meet the student's needs in unique ways. One person, for example, may be concerned with the cognitive part; another, with the affective part of the interaction.

Many-to-many is exemplified by the team-taught class or seminar, in which several faculty teach by working together. This may involve many parallel or sequential one-to-one interactions. Having other faculty present adds more feedback, more evaluation and communication between the different faculty members, as well as between teachers and students. These experiences may be very educational, helpful, and meaningful to the students. They also may be very frustrating and time-consuming.

All cases of mechanical and other nonhuman processes include books, maps, atlases, and other devices. Some of these may be organized in programmed instruction, such as scrambled books, teaching books, teaching machines, and other well-known formats. The advent of new media adds a great variety of one-way communication devices—including filmstrips, video tapes, tape recordings, records, slides, and movies—which are used to present information in serial and, at times, parallel fashion. Interactive devices like computer-assisted instruction, trainers, simulators, and other devices in which the student gets interacting feedback in his learning are coming into use. The importance of large groupings of such devices cannot be underestimated. These include language centers, libraries, and laboratories, where groups of many devices may be used with one or many students, who may share them or use them sequentially. The understanding of the effects of the environment on students is barely grasped and not studied extensively (Rath, 1968).

Beyond all of these effects, the theory for teaching should be able to deal with the interactions of systems and their sequential effects. For example, what is the interaction of different subjects which students study? Is the studying of English before math any better than studying math before English, or does this depend on the student? What is the impact of having several students studying together, and should they be studying the same thing or different things? Interactions over time and space are important. Interactions, in effect, between the students, faculty, environment, and the various teaching devices are important. A theory for teaching, therefore, has to describe the current state of the system; determine the desired future states; and develop methods of getting from the current state to the desired state. If this can be done successfully and humanistically we have succeeded in developing a useful theory for teaching.

> "There is nothing as practical as a good theory."
>
> KURT LEWIN.

REFERENCES

Bennis, W., Schein, E., Steele, F., and Berlew, D. "Personal Change Through Interpersonal Relationships." In *Interpersonal Dynamics:*

Essays and Readings on Human Interaction, ed. Warren G. Bennis, rev. ed. Homewood, Ill. : Dorsey Press, 1969. Pp. 333-369.

Churchman, C. W. *The Systems Approach.* New York : Delacorte Press, 1968.

Mesarovic, M., Macko, D., and Takahara, Y. *Theory of Hierarchical, Multi-level Systems.* New York : Academic Press, 1970.

Miller, J. G. and Rath, G. J. "Planning-Programming-Budgeting and Cost-Effectiveness in Educational Systems." In *To Improve Learning: An Evaluation of Instructional Technology,* ed. S. G. Tickton. New York : R. R. Bowker Company, 1971. Pp. 1029-1060.

Rath, G. J. "Carrels and the Disadvantaged Child," *Educational Product Report,* Vol. 2, No. 2 (1968), pp. 20-21.

Rath, G. J. "The School and the School System." Sections in J. G. Miller, "The Living Systems Involved in the Educational Process," in *To Improve Learning: An Evaluation of Instructional Technology,* ed. S. G. Tickton, Vol. II. New York : R. R. Bowker Company, 1971. Pp. 261-270.

Slobin, Dan I., ed. *The Ontagenesis of Grammar: A Theoretical Symposium.* New York : Academic Press, 1971.

Thompson, C. W. N. and Rath, G. J. "The Administrative Experiment : A Special Case of Field Testing or Evaluation." In *Human Factors* (in press).

Index

Abstraction, experience and, 55
Alliances, *see* Dogmatic alliances; Erotic alliances; Ethnographic alliance; Existential alliances; Humanistic alliance; Intellectual alliances; Learning alliance; Moral alliance; Pragmatic alliances; Therapeutic alliance
Allport, Gordon W., 36n
Alternatives in systems analysis, 144
  examples of, 145, 147
Analytic or critical philosophy, 12-13
Anderson, R., 125-26
Anthropology, 82; *see also* Ethnographic alliance
Authoritarian education, 44-45
Axioms in hypothetico-deductive model, 15

Bantum, Nila, 124-25
Bargain-making, learning alliance and, 92, 94-96
Barzun, Jacques, 106
Bateson, Gregory, 81
Behavior
  functional analysis of, 36
  objective viewpoint in observation of, 16-17
  operant, 37n
  respondent (reflexive), 37n
Behavioral objectives
  observational categories and, 69-71
  perceptual learning and, 69-75
Behavioral sciences, *see* Social Sciences
Behaviorism
  perceptual categories and, 60, 61
  psychoanalytic school compared to, 42, 45n
  theories of learning and teaching in, 36-40, 48-50
Bennis, Warren G., 169
  model of personal change developed by, 154
  on qualities concerned with extension of identity or self-image, 129-30
Berlew, David E., 130n, 169
Bettelheim, Bruno
  on psychoanalytic approach to education, 44-45

Bettelheim, Bruno, cont'd
  therapeutic learning alliances and, 104
Broad, C. D., 12-13
Buber, Martin, 108

Cantril, H., 121
Center for the Teaching Professions (Northwestern University), 2-3
Change, models for personal, 154
Churchman, C. W., 140, 170
Classification of experience, 55-56
Classroom as system, 139; *see also* Systems approach to the theory for teaching
Classroom structures, individualized, 123-130
Coleman, James A., 24
Computer-assisted instruction systems, 141-42
Computers as information storage source, 142
Concept formation in systems analysis, 154-57, 159
Conception, perceptual categories and, 58-61
Conditioning, operant
  deprivation phase of, 94-95
  of verbal behavior, 150-51
Conferences, scheduling teacher-student, 135-36
Conflict
  inner, therapeutic learning alliances and, 104
  systems
    in ethnographic alliance, 82-87
    in learning alliance, 87-96
    systems analysis and, 161
    in therapeutic alliance, 76-82
Constraints and resources in systems analysis, 142, 144
  examples of, 146, 148
Control, positive reinforcement as counterproductive when used to achieve, 94-95
Controlling a class, learning alliance and, 88-96
Coody, Betty, 123n
Cotton, John W., 32n

Countertransference in therapeutic alliance, 76, 79, 96
Criteria in systems analysis, 142
  example of, 145, 146
Critical or analytic philosophy, 12-13
Culture, perceptual capacities and, 55
Culture shock, 76, 84-87, 96

Dame School, 124-25
Decision-making, systems analysis and, 142, 144
Deductive logic, 15
  inferring *oughts* from ontological or empirical premises as violation of, 27
  See also Hypothetico-deductive model
Determinism
  of behaviorism, 37, 42
  of psychoanalytic theory, 41-42
Deutero-learning, 81
Dewey, Evelyn, 25
Dewey, John, 13, 25, 107
  on individual variations, 122
  Pedagogic Creed of, 27
Dogmatic alliances, 99, 100, 104-5

Ego, the, 43
Ego strength, 43-45
Einstein, Albert, 31, 163
  theory as defined by, 30
Empathy
  openness in concept formation and, 155, 156
  subjective viewpoint and, 17, 20
Empirical research, 10
Environment in systems approach, 139-40
Erikson, Eric, 165
Erotic alliances, 99, 100, 102-3
  matching learner needs and teaching style in, 108-12
Esalen Institute, 103
Ethnographic alliance, 76, 82-87
  culture shock and, 84-85
  relevance for teachers of, 85-87
  systems analysis and, 161
Evaluation conferences, scheduling, 135-36
Evaluation procedure or model in systems analysis, 144
  examples of, 146, 147
Existential alliances, 99, 100, 107-8

Existentialism, individual differences in perceived values and, 121-22
Experience, abstraction and classification of, 55-56

Facilitators, teachers as, 128-30
  Rogers' concept of, 21, 22, 47-48, 138
Falsifiability, scientific theory and, 15-16
Fox, R. S., 127
Fraenkel, Jack, 24n
Free schools, 47
Freeman, F. S., 123
Freud, Sigmund
  determinism of, 42n
  psychoanalytic theory of, 40-42, 163
Fromm, Erich, 42n
Fundamentalist revival, dogmatic learning alliances and, 104-5

Galileo, 15
Gestalt psychology, erotic learning alliances and, 102-3
Goal systems conflict, learning alliance and, 89-96
Green, Thomas F., 11n, 34
Greenspoon, J., 150
Gripe sessions, 136
Gross, Richard F., 23n
Group discussions, scheduling, 135, 136
Group projects
  individual differences and, 133-34
  scheduling of, 135-36
Guidance movement, 103-04
Guilt, dogmatic learning alliances and relief from, 104, 105
Guthrie, E. R., 165

Hall, Calvin, 41n
Hanson, Norwood R., 14n, 62n
Harris, Ben M., 123n
Hempel, C. G., 14n, 15n
Hierarchies, perceptual, 58, 62-65, 75
  ground-floor levels of perception and, 64-65, 160
Homework, perceptual learning and, 73
Hook, Sidney, 27
Horney, Karen, on psychoanalysts' observations, 155-56
Human potential movement, 102, 103
Humanistic approach to education, psychological aspects of, 45-50, 103-4

INDEX

Humanistic alliance, 99, 100, 103-4
Hume, David, 27
Hutchins, Robert, 106
Hypothetico-deductive model, 14-16
   schematic form of, 15
   systems analysis and, 159

Id, the, 43
Identity, qualities concerned with extension of, 129-30
Identity crisis, humanistic approach to, 103
Individual differences, influence on instructional theories of, 118-38
   administrative or organizational machinery, influence of, 125-26
   classroom structures, individualized, 123-30
   divergent responses to individual differences, 122-23
   interactional process, influence of, 126-28
   knowledge, differences in, 120-21
   perceived values, differences in, 121-22
   reality and categories of individual differences, 120
   social demands, differences in, 122
   specific interpersonal techniques used to respond to individual differences, 130-38
      assessment of differences, 131
      conveying respect for individual uniquenesses, 132-33
      group projects, 133-34
      planning instruction, 131-32
      promoting sensitivity to individual differences, 137-38
      time schedule, 134-37
   systems analysis and, 162
   teacher's role and responsibility in, 128-30
Infeld, Leopold, $30n$
Inner conflict, therapeutic learning alliances and, 104
Instruction
   definition of, 34
   theory of, 33-34
Intellectual alliances, 99, 100, 106-7
Interpersonal knowing, Rogers' concept of, 20
Interpersonal techniques, *see under* Individual differences, influence on instructional theories of
Ittelson, W., $121n$

"Jesus freaks," 104
Jones, Richard M., 104

Kant, Immanuel, 57
Kaplan, Abraham, 10
King, Martin Luther, 13
Klemke, E. D., $62n$
Knowledge, individual differences in, 120-21
Knowledge process, systems analysis and, 153-58
Koffka, K., $62n$
Kohler, W., $62n$
Krantz, David L., $36n$
Kuhn, Thomas S., 9, $62n$, $152n$

Learning
   perceptual, *see* Perceptual learning
   proto- and deutero-, 81
   theories of, theories for teaching and, 32, 48-50; *see also under* Learning alliance
Learning alliance, 7, 87-117
   bargain making in, 92, 94-96
   controlling a class and, 88-96
   criteria for evaluating alternative perspectives on, 112-17
   dogmatic, 99, 100, 104-5
   erotic, 99, 100, 102-3
      matching learner needs and teaching style in, 108-12
   existential, 99, 100, 107-8
   humanistic, 99, 100, 103-4
   intellectual, 99, 100, 106-7
   learner's discontent, alternative alliances against, 99-101
   moral, 99, 100, 105-6
      matching learner needs and teaching style in, 108-12
   "nonrelationships" and, 101
   pragmatic, 99, 100, 107
      matching learner needs and teaching style in, 108-12
   systems conflict in, 87-96
   therapeutic, 99, 100, 104
   therapeutic alliance's relevance to, 88-89

Learning alliance cont'd
  unwillingness of students to enter, 80
  usefulness test for, 108-12
Lewin, Kurt, 8, 154, 169
Lindzey, Gardner, 41n
Locke, John, 14
Logic
  deductive, 15
    inferring *oughts* from ontological or empirical premises as violation of, 27
    See also Hypothetico-deductive model
  as tool of theory-building, 10
Luszki, M. B., 127n

Mabry, John, 39n
McGaghie, William C., 3
Machines, teaching, positive reinforcement of learner by, 18-19
Macko, D., 170
McPhie, Walter E., 23n
Magenoff, Milton, 138n
Martin, Jane R., 59n
Marxism, moral learning alliance and, 106
Maslow, A. H., 165
Mathis, B. Claude, 3, 32n, 59
Meaning, human, subjective vs. objective viewpoints and, 19-20
Mesarovic, M., 140, 170
Michael, J., 38-39
Mill, John S., 16
Miller, J. G., 140, 170
Models in systems analysis, 157-60
  evaluation of theories through, 164
  theories compared to, 149-51
Moral education, 71-72
Moral alliance, 99, 100, 105-6
  matching learner needs and teaching style in, 108-12
Morris, Van Cleve, 121-22
Motivation
  behaviorist approach to, 40
  psychoanalytic approach to, 45
Mowat, Farley, 9

Natural sciences
  social sciences' relationship to, 16-17
  See also Physical sciences

Newton, Sir Isaac, 15
Nongraded schools, 125-26
Northwestern University, 4
  Center for the Teaching Professions at, 2-3
Nyberg, David, 65-68, 72

Objective viewpoint of scientific theories of teaching, 17-22
  subjective viewpoint contrasted to, 20-22
Objectives in systems analysis, 142
  examples of, 145, 146, 148
Observation
  knowledge process and, 155-56
  participant, 82-83
Observational categories, behavioral objectives, perceptual learning and, 69-71
  systems approach and, 160
Olson, Willard C., 125
Ontological presuppositions, practical role of theory and, 25-27
Openness, knowledge process and, 154-56, 161
Operant behavior, 37n
Operant conditioning
  deprivation phase of, 94-95
  of verbal behavior, 150-51
Oppenheim, Paul, 15n
Organismic valuing process, Rogers' concept of, 21

Participant observation, 82-83
Perception
  ground-floor levels of, 64-65
  relating theory to, 65-69
  teaching and, 58; *see also* Perceptual learning
Perceptual capacities, 53-56
Perceptual categories
  conception and, 58-61
  hierarchies of, 62-65
  learning, *see* Perceptual learning
Perceptual hierarchies, 58, 62-65, 75
  ground-floor levels of perception and, 64-65, 160
Perceptual learning
  "affective" modes of teaching and, 74-75
  behavioral objectives, teaching strategies and, 69-75

INDEX

Perceptual learning cont'd
 implications for the teacher, 71-75
 homework and, 73
 moral education and, 71-72
 need for, 56-58
 relating theory to practice in, 65-69
Perls, Fritz, 103
Personal change, model of, 154
Personality development,
  psychoanalytic approach to, 44, 45
Petrie, Hugh G., 62n, 70n
Philosophy
 analytical or critical, 12-13
 of education, 25-27
 speculative, 13
Physical sciences
 practical role of theory in, 23, 24
 theory as defined in, 12
 See also Natural sciences
Plato, 12, 13
Polanyi, Michael, 9, 83, 153n
Popper, K. R., 14n, 15
Positive regard, concept of, 103
Positive reinforcement, 18, 22, 37n
 as counterproductive when used to achieve control, 94-95
 in operant conditioning of verbal behavior, 150-51
Powell, W., 120
Powers, William, 62n
Pragmatic alliances, 99, 100, 107
 matching learner needs and teaching style in, 108-12
Prediction, hypothetico-deductive model and, 16
Problem formulation in systems analysis, 142
 examples of, 145, 146
Progress conferences, scheduling, 135-36
Proto-learning, 81
Psychoanalysts
 Horney on observations by, 155-56
 in therapeutic alliance, *see* Therapeutic alliances
Psychoanalytic theory of education, 40-45, 48-50
 behaviorism compared to, 42, 45n
Psychology
 Gestalt, erotic learning alliances and, 102-3
 teaching theories from perspective of, 35-50
 behaviorism, 36-40, 42, 45n, 48-50
 humanistic approach, 45-50
 psychoanalytic theory, 40-45
 theories of learning and, 48-50
Psychosexual development, in psychoanalytic theory, 42-43

Quine, W. V. O., 62n

Radical social and political criticism, moral learning alliances and, 105-6
Rath, Gustave J., 140, 154, 169, 170
Rebellion of students, learning alliance and, 88-96
Redemption, dogmatic learning alliance and, 104-5
Redfield, Robert, 23-25, 28
Reflexive behavior, 37n
Reinforcement
 environmental contingencies of, 37-38, 40
 negative, 37n, 94
 positive, 18, 22, 37n
  as counterproductive when used to achieve control, 94-95
  in operant conditioning of verbal behavior, 150-51
Resources and constraints in systems analysis, 142, 144
 examples of, 146, 148
Respondent behavior, 37n
Reward
 as counterproductive when used to achieve control, 94-95
 See also Reinforcement—positive
Rogers, Carl, 122
 on empathic understanding, 155
 humanistic approach of, 46-48, 103-4, 113
 on operant conditioning of verbal behavior, 150-51
 subjective viewpoint of theory of teaching of, 20-22
 teachers-as-facilitators concept of, 21, 22, 47-48, 138
 on teacher characteristics that facilitate awareness, 129
Role playing, perceptual learning and, 74-75

Rosseau, Jean Jacques, 13
  Emile, 25-26
Rudner, Richard, 56n
Russell, Bertrand, 13
Ryle, Gilbert, 13

Savetsky, M., 125
Scenarios in systems analysis, 144
Schedule, individual differences and, 134-137
Schein, Edgar H., 130n, 169
Schmuch, R., 127n
Science, *see* Natural sciences; Physical sciences; Social sciences
Scientific theories for teaching, 12
  objective viewpoint in, 16-19
  practical role of theory in, 25-29, 159
  subjective viewpoint in, 19-22
Scientific theory (in general), 12-16
  falsifiable hypotheses in, 15-16
  hypothetico-deductive model of, *see* Hypothetico-deductive model
  "non scientific" vs., 12-13
  practical role of, 23
  predictive capacity of, 16
  systems analysis and, 148-53
    active nature of both, 151-52
    highly personal nature of both, 152-53
    models and theories compared, 149-51, 159
Sechrest, Lee, 32n
Self-actualization, humanistic approach to, 46-48
Self-definition, humanistic approach to, 103
Self-directed activity, interactional process and, 132-33
Self-image, qualities concerned with extension of, 129-30
Sensitivity training, perceptual learning and, 74-75
Sexual development, psychoanalytic theory and, 42-43
Shane, Harold G., 122n
Silberman, Charles, 11
Simon, Herbert, 149
Skinner, B. F., 14, 40n, 60, 94, 113, 165
  objective theory of teaching of, 18-19, 22
  on objective viewpoint in behavioral science, 17

Skinner, B. F. cont'd
  as radical behaviorist, 18
  reinforcement theory of, 18, 22, 36-37
Slobin, Dan I., 151, 170
Smith, N. B., 125n
Social sciences
  natural sciences' relationship to, 16-17
  practical role of theory in, 23-25
  theories in, 31-32
Sociology, Weber on subjective viewpoint in, 19-20
Socratic tradition, 12
Speculative philosophy, 13
Stachnick, Thomas, 39n
Steele, Fred I., 130n, 169
Strategies, teaching, perceptual learning and, 69-75
Subjective viewpoint of scientific theory for teaching, 19-22
Superego, the, 43
Systems approach to the theory for teaching, 139-70
  assumptions of, 139
  description of systems thinking in, 140-42
  entities that a theory of teaching must account for, 165-69
    one-to-one, one-to-many, many-to-one and many-to-many relationships, 167-68
  environment's role in, 139-40
  input to and output from system in, 139-40
  open vs. closed systems, 140-41
  systems analysis in, 142-65
    concept formation, 154-57, 159
    examples, 145-48
    ideal systems analyst, description of, 158
    as knowledge process, 148, 153-58
    models in, *see* Models in systems analysis
    openness and, 154-56, 161
    paradigm and outlines of process, 142-45
    relationship of other chapters in this book to framework of, 158-63
    scientific theory and, *see* Scientific theory—systems analysis and
    use of theory in, 163-64
    use of theories of, 164-65
Systems conflict, *see* Conflict—systems

INDEX

Takahara, Y., 170
Teaching
  concept of, 11-12
  theories for, *see* Theories for teaching
  See also specific topics
Teaching-learning alliance, *see* Learning alliance
Teaching machines, positive reinforcement of learner by, 18-19
Teaching strategies, perceptual learning and, 69-75
Technology of teaching, 18
Thelen, Lewin Herbert, 128n
Theorems in hypothetico-deductive model, 15
Theories for teaching
  individuality of participants in learning situation and, *see* Individual differences, influence on instructional theories of
  introduction to, 2-3, 5-6
  psychological perspectives for, 35-50
    behaviorism, 36-40, 42, 45n, 48-50
    humanistic approach, 45-50
    psychoanalytic theory, 40-45
    theories of learning, 48-50
  scientific, *see* Scientific theories for teaching
  systems approach to, *see* Systems approach to the theory of learning
  theory building process and, 33-35
  theory of learning and, 32, 48-50
Theory (in general)
  definitions of
    Einstein's, 30
    Kaplan's, 10
    in physical sciences, 12
    as structural framework for empirical investigation, 31
    vagueness of, 12
  expilicit vs. implicit, 10
  lawful relations in structure of, 31
  perceptual experience and, 55

Theory (in general) cont'd
  scientific, *see* Scientific theory (in general)
  systems analysis use of, 163-64
Therapeutic alliance, 76-82
  blind spots in, 78-79
  initial intervention in, 78
  rebellion of patient in, 88-89
  supervision of therapists in, 78-79
  teacher-student relationship and, 79-82, 88-89; *see also* Therapeutic teaching-learning alliance
Therapeutic teaching-learning alliance, 99, 100, 104
Thompson, C. W. N., 154, 170
Thorndike, E. L., 36n
Tickton, S. G., 170
Toilet training, 42-43
Toulmin, Stephen, 62n
Training, concept of, perceptual categories and, 59-61
Transference, therapeutic, 78, 79, 104
Travers, Robert M. W., 34n

Ulrich, Roger, 39n

Values
  individual differences in perceived, 121-22
  in Rogers' theory of organismic valuing process, 21
  social sciences' relationship to social, 24-25
Valuing process, organismic, 21
Van Lawick-Goodall, Jane, 9
Veatch, J., 125
Verban behavior, operant conditioning of, 150-51
Verplanck, 150

Watson, John B., 16
Weber, Max, 19-20
Wittgenstein, Ludwig, 52n, 62n